# THE GAME CHANGERS

# THE GAME CHANGERS

SUCCESS SECRETS FROM INSPIRATIONAL WOMEN
CHANGING THE GAME AND INFLUENCING THE WORLD

SAMANTHA BRETT   STEPH ADAMS

VIKING
*an imprint of*
PENGUIN BOOKS

VIKING

UK | USA | Canada | Ireland | Australia
India | New Zealand | South Africa | China

Penguin Books is part of the Penguin Random House group of companies
whose addresses can be found at global.penguinrandomhouse.com.

Penguin
Random House
Australia

First published by Fearless Femmes Pty Ltd, 2017
This revised edition published by Penguin Random House Australia Pty Ltd, 2017

Cover design by Steph Adams.
Text design by Steph Adams.
Colour separation by Splitting Image Colour Studio, Clayton, Victoria
Printed and bound in China by RR Donnelley Asia Printing Solutions Ltd

National Library of Australia Cataloguing-in-Publication data is available.

ISBN 9780143787723


penguin.com.au

*This book is dedicated to all the Game Changers
in the world who aren't afraid to go after their causes,
goals and dreams no matter what challenges they face
along the way. We salute you and stand by you.*

*To my daughter, Harper, may all your dreams come true,
may you never be afraid to change the game and be
fearless in all your pursuits. Never be scared to take on
challenges no matter how difficult they may seem, do not let
those who try to put you down get in your way, and may you
always strive to become any woman you would like to
be – no matter what path you choose.* **Samantha Brett**

*I would like to dedicate this book to my beautiful friend
Annaliesse Thompson Passmore, who lost her battle to breast
cancer. She will always be one of the most amazing women
I have ever had the privilege of knowing. A beautiful friend
taken too soon, who had a love for life and sense of humour
to match. I will miss you every day.* **Steph Adams**

# Game Changer:

/geɪm/ /ˈtʃeɪn(d)ʒə/

noun

a person who effects a significant shift in the current way of doing
or thinking about something

believes in own ideas and doesn't accept rejection, naysayers or negativity

turns ideas into reality and supports others endeavouring to do the same

Photo credit: Chantelli Bianchi, Makeup by: Priya Noble and Juliana Stojanovska. Clothes worn here by Carla Zampatti

# CONTENTS

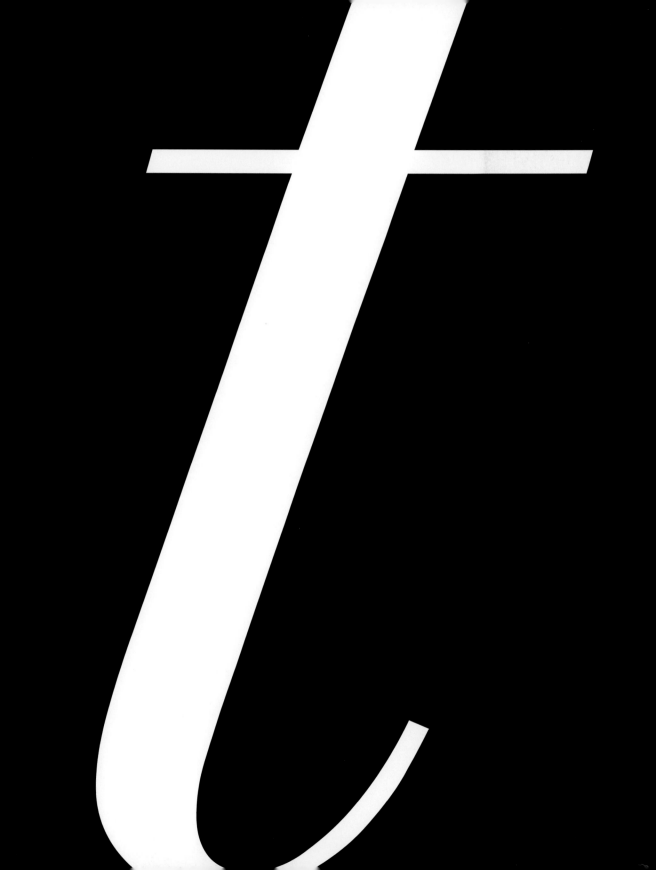

*THERE ARE STILL MANY CAUSES WORTH SACRIFICING FOR, SO MUCH HISTORY YET TO BE MADE*

**MICHELLE OBAMA**

# INTRODUCTION

Today, women in the developed world are better placed than ever before. We have more opportunities, better treatment in the workplace, more rights, greater respect and are kicking goals in boardrooms and situation rooms across the globe. But there is still a great divide. As Facebook COO and women's advocate Sheryl Sandberg duly notes, 'The blunt truth is that men still run the world,' despite what Beyoncé might croon. Senator Hillary Clinton agrees, telling a Women for Women International luncheon in 2017 that 'women's rights are the unfinished business of the 21st century'.

Arianna Huffington tells us her story of running for Governor of California, where she was confronted with 'the fear of being caricatured and misunderstood' as a woman in politics. How she quickly realised how much harder it would be running for the top job as a woman, feeling so much more exposed and vulnerable than her opponent, Arnold Schwarzenegger. And yet, she refused to back down despite the odds, pushing forward and becoming a role model for women the world over for simply giving it a go.

We all know the facts: women work just as hard – if not harder – than their male counterparts. Not to mention the fact women are expected to have kids, look after the home, cook the meals and make sure their partners are happy, all the while holding down a full-time job because heck, modern women can indeed 'have it all'. And yet so many women are not being compensated for it. In fact, according to the World Economic Forum's 2016 Global Gender Gap Report, it would take around 170 years to achieve economic parity between the genders! As two mothers who hope our children will be unafraid to follow their passions and dreams, to us this is unacceptable. Something has to change.

But this isn't a book filled with musings over the unfair treatment of women in the workplace. Instead this book is a celebration of female achievements, a testament to the women we know and love – and their strength, determination, successes and ability to do incredible things despite the purported pay gap and alleged glass ceiling. Women who continue to pick themselves up and keep going, especially when the going gets tough.

Through our roles in the media, television and publishing industries, we have spent more than two decades combined interviewing some of the world's most inspirational women – and we have noticed a recurring message: never give up. The women featured in this book have let us behind the scenes of the glitz and glamour of their seemingly easy career trajectories, and detailed their personal struggles, hardships and challenges along the way to help you, dear reader, follow your dreams too.

From the stories you're about to read in these pages, you'll learn that being a Game Changer is all about falling, failing, and then getting up after you've fallen down; trying one more time when you feel like every avenue has been exhausted, sending out one more resume, doing one more round of emails … especially when you feel like you do not have the strength to try anymore. Because being a Game Changer isn't about having the best idea or the most money or being the smartest person in the room – it's about never giving up, especially when you want to.

*Sam & Steph*
xx

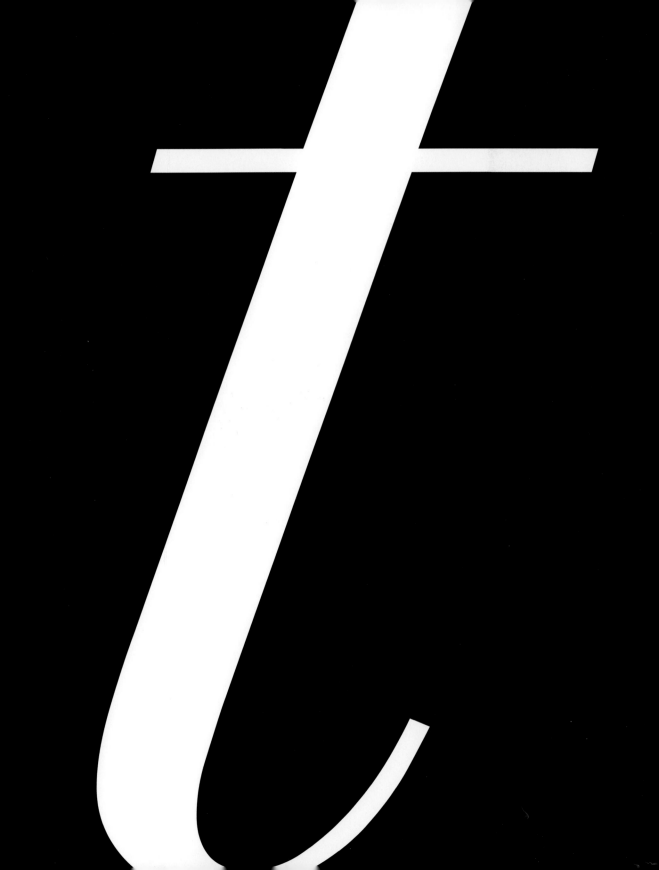

# the GAME CHANGING RULES

# TOP TEN TIPS TO CREATE YOUR OWN GAME CHANGING BRAND

**YOUR BRILLIANT IDEA**

Game Changing brands have identified a missing or much-needed product or service, and have gone out and created it. Or they've looked at a popular product or service and worked out a way to do it better. Either way, they have picked a niche that they are passionate about and are willing to put in the long hours and hard yards to make it a success. If you are stuck on how to find your brilliant idea, close your eyes and think back to a time in your life when you were most happy. What were you doing? Where were you working? Visualise this scenario clearly and frequently, and then start brainstorming. You'll be surprised by the business ideas that will flow.

**SCOUT YOUR COMPETITION**

Game Changers are aware of their competition, but do not dwell on it. They know there is room for everyone at the top. They know they might have a different audience or niche, or better way of doing things, and they don't let a little friendly competition get in their way. They know that their passion will surpass anyone in their space and they aren't afraid to pound the pavement to achieve their dreams.

**KNOW YOUR TARGET MARKET**

The better you know your target market, the more successful you are going to be. Research what your audience needs, likes, how they spend, who they hang out with, what social media sites they follow. Know them intimately so you can cater your business to fulfilling their needs.

**WORK OUT HOW YOU'RE GOING TO MAKE MONEY**

It's all very well having a passion project, but work out how you're going to monetise what you're offering. There are a number of revenue streams available to you, whether it be through advertising on a blog, selling a product, offering a service or creating a subscription model.

**SETTING UP THE BUSINESS**

Now that you know what you're offering and how you're going to make money, the next step is to actually set it up! If you're looking at opening a bricks and mortar store, you're going to need builders, architects, plumbers and so on. If you're looking at starting an online business, you're going to need the equivalent in the online world: a website builder, an SEO specialist, marketing and sales channels. A great tool for affordable logos and starter websites is fiverr.com – simply put up your project description and see the offers roll in at affordable prices. You can always hire a big development firm at a later stage after you have proof of concept.

## SOCIAL MEDIA

You'll need to become a pro at tooting your own horn and, thanks to the explosion of social media, it's free to start a Facebook and Instagram page for your business, which studies show is currently the best form of marketing. You no longer have to spend big bucks on television advertisements to get noticed! Look at our Instagram tips in the following pages and set something up that will bring customers to you. Link your Instagram to your Facebook page so everything you do is on brand and in sync – and make sure it all links back to your website which has a clear description of how to buy your products or engage your service.

## EXPANDING YOUR BRAND

Once you've established your brand, becoming a true Game Changer is about thinking outside the box. Partner with other brands to expand your customer base, write an ebook or book giving advice about your niche, start a blog – the choices and expansion opportunities are endless. The stories in this book prove that no Game Changer follows the same path; what they do share is a narrow and targeted focus and obsession with making whatever their chosen path is a success.

## GET NOTICED

Hiring a public relations consultant is expensive and time consuming, and is a great tool to use when your business starts to make some serious cash. But when you're just starting out, you still want to get noticed while spending a minimum amount on marketing. Good news is you can easily contact producers of television morning shows to pitch a segment idea based on your product or service. You can purchase Instagram and Facebook advertising. And you can use a service such as Tribe, which allows businesses to scout for social influencers who can then spread the word about your product or service. It is worth looking at a high profile ambassador who can spread the world as well; as you will notice this is a tool used by many of the Game Changers we interviewed.

## BE CONSISTENT

Game Changing businesses that offer a product, do so with great consistency. They have good branding, packaging, customer service, web presence and brand awareness. They treat every customer as though they are their only customer and know that the customer always come first, even when they're being difficult! Look at how you can make your customer experience better and always look for innovative ways to improve.

## LEARN FROM YOUR MISTAKES

Every Game Changer you'll read about in this book has made mistakes and picked themselves back up and started again. Do not let failure (or the fear of failure) get in your way. Ask for help when you need it; hire someone who is better than you to take care of the details that you can't and remember, Rome wasn't built in a day. Creating a successful Game Changing brand takes time and persistence. But believe in what you are doing and you will achieve.

# HOW TO STAY BALANCED

*Staying balanced when you are juggling a career, business, staff, packaging, couriers, customers, web developers … not to mention kids, a husband, (or embarking on the search for a partner!), parents, siblings and pets is no mean feat. Life can get off kilter pretty quickly. A key element to many of our Game Changers' roads to success is their continual quest to stay balanced. It's no easy feat. But following the advice from the women we've polled, here are some of their top tips to help you keep your centre and make sure you have time to smell the roses.*

**LEARN TO SAY NO**

We are often told to 'say yes' to every opportunity in order to become successful at whatever we're attempting to achieve. But juggling too many things at once can often mean that balls get dropped. Very good advice we were once given is to concentrate on one thing, and to do it well. News presenter Melissa Doyle agrees, and tells us her key tip to juggling her multitude of roles is, 'Don't try to do everything'. Instead, she talks of learning to say no as being instrumental in helping her being able to fit in the things that are most important to her. Saying no doesn't mean that you've failed; it means that you're prioritising what is vital to the growth of your career or business and being confident enough to say no to the things that you aren't able to give your best to.

**DEDICATE TIME**

One Game Changer we know finished writing an entire novel while working full-time in an office job by doing an hour of writing every morning before the sun rose. Another used every lunch break during her day-job to work on her business plan – and before long was able to quit her job to work on her now multi-million dollar business. If you work best in the mornings, get up early and dedicate an hour each morning to chipping away at something you've long been meaning to get done. The same if you're a night person; incredible things can be achieved by setting aside a dedicated hour a day.

**TAKE TIME OUT**

While dedicating time to your business is imperative for it to grow, equally important is allocating time to nourish your soul. Even ten minutes a day can be all it takes to stop you from burning out. Take the time out to go for a walk, meditate, travel, write in your gratitude journal (it sounds airy-fairy but it really works!), do some yoga moves, phone a friend overseas, do some baking – whatever it is that soothes your soul and helps you to switch your mind off from the daily grind.

**NOURISH YOURSELF**

In the world of fad diets and quick fixes, nutritionists are now offering some very simple

*Steph Adams in the Maldives*

advice: eat. There is no harm in quitting sugar (see Sarah Wilson's inspiring story) or going organic and adding green juices to your daily routine (see Jessica Sepel's incredible health journey), but when life gets in the way, modern women are often doing one pivotal thing wrong: they are forgetting to eat altogether, preferring to grab a coffee instead. But not eating not only slows down your metabolism: it can make you moody, your brain foggy and cause you to make rash decisions, simply because you are so darn hungry! There are simple, easy fixes to not having enough time to eat, including online grocery shopping and a bevy of healthy delivery meal services. Not to mention you can actually lose weight by eating more as it keeps your metabolism moving – as long as it's more of the right foods.

## SWEAT

When entrepreneurs get really busy, the first thing to go is health and exercise. But even the busiest CEOs and Game Changers we interviewed told us they make sure they find the time to fit in exercising as it not only helps their bodies, but their minds as well. Whether it's a 5 a.m. jog by the ocean, a weekend Pilates class or a mid-week lunchtime boxing session, it's important to sweat at least a few times a week.

## DON'T FORGET YOUR LOVED ONES

No success is worth it without being surrounded by those you love. Schedule a monthly dinner with girlfriends or a weekly date night with your partner no matter how busy you get. There's always room for recharging the batteries. And a good old-fashioned laugh with friends is the best cure for every woe.

*BEING FEARLESS ISN'T BEING 100 PER CENT NOT FEARFUL, IT'S BEING TERRIFIED BUT YOU JUMP ANYWAY*

**TAYLOR SWIFT**

# HOW TO PREPARE FOR A JOB INTERVIEW

**KNOW YOUR COMPANY**

Knowing everything about where you are applying to work will instantly put you at the top of the pile. Research their latest projects, company goals, staff structure and company motto.

**BE THE PART**

One Game Changing woman told us she always carries a copy of the *Washington Post* newspaper with her on the day of her job interview. That way, not only is she up to speed on current events, but it is a great conversation starter, an excellent way to show she isn't just about appearances, and a tell-tale sign that she is all about business.

**LOOK THE PART**

You'd be surprised how many people actually forget to change outfits for a job interview! Unless you're going for a job at an activewear store, dress to impress. Keep your hemlines long, makeup clean and fresh, shirts ironed and immaculate, and add a funky accessory if you're going for a job at a fashion label. Same with hair and nails – clean, neat, fresh and polished.

**BRING YOUR RESUME AND HAVE IT READY**

There is nothing worse than rummaging through your oversized, over-packed handbag while an executive is watching you get redder and redder in the face. Have everything you need ready to go. If you have a portfolio, carry it in your hand. If you have a video, have your memory stick connected to your keyring so you can simply whack it into your interviewer's computer. And make sure it works!

**DON'T BE AFRAID TO ASK QUESTIONS**

The more you know about the company, the more intelligent a question you can ask. You only need one or two to show your interviewer that you're genuinely interested in working for the company and getting to know more about it. Steer away from questions about lunch breaks or discounts! Instead, ask something about what they're looking for in a candidate or where they see room for growth in the company.

**FOLLOW UP**

Send a follow-up email after your interview letting the interviewer know it was lovely to meet them and you look forward to hearing back. Be patient when waiting for a response. And don't put all your eggs into one basket. Keep applying for other positions – and keep your options open and varied.

# HOW TO BUILD A LOYAL INSTAGRAM FOLLOWING

*Even if you're technologically challenged, everyone can use Instagram – it's that simple! And if you want to grow your brand or business, we strongly advise you jump on the rapidly growing trend. After all, the mobile phone app has 500 million active users every month, and 95 million photos and videos are shared across the platform every day. Studies have found that Instagram provides brands with 25 per cent more engagement than other marketing platforms so it's definitely worth your while not only to jump on board, but to do it in style.*

### HIGH QUALITY PHOTOS

Always post high quality photos that are interesting and engaging to your audience. Keep photos clear and bright. You'll see the more experienced influencers carrying around high-tech cameras. They'll then edit their photos using Photoshop before posting them to Instagram. If you would rather use your phone, download an app that uses the flashlight setting. This will enable you to get good lighting in your photo, without an orange hue from a flash. If using an iPhone, take your Instagram pics using the square setting so you don't have to crop them later.

### BE GENUINE AND DON'T OVER EDIT

Try to post as many of your own photos, artwork and flat lays as possible, and if you are posting the work of others, always credit them and state why you posted it. Be genuine in the way you tell your own story. You do not have to overly edit your photos or put too many filters on them. The best posts are the ones that use true colours and textures. Of course there are a number of tools you can use to enhance your posts including the sharpen tool, exposure, shadows and clarity. Play around with the edit tools and filters and see what suits your style best.

### POST MINIMUM 2–3 TIMES PER WEEK

Always keep your audience coming back for more. Post two to three times minimum per week, or three times a day at most (if you can!).

## TAKE NOTE OF YOUR BACKGROUND

Your background is extremely important. Try to keep it from being too busy. A clean and crisp white background will give your posts a professional feel. You can use a kitchen bench top, a bed sheet or a white piece of cardboard from an art shop for a professional looking flat lay. For shots out and about, make sure the lighting is natural and coming from the front of your object rather than behind. Look for interesting backgrounds too. Beautiful tiles, a big rock, a gorgeous floor… There's beauty everywhere if you crop it, edit it and caption it correctly!

## USE RELEVANT HASHTAGS

Hashtags that relate to your location or topic will help others to find you and get your photo noticed. Research what hashtags are popular in the genre of your business. Try to use unique hashtags as well to keep your posts different from your competitors.

## COLLABORATE WITH VARIOUS BRANDS

Collaborating with various brands will help to get your photo regrammed and get you noticed by their own audience. Reach out to brands you think will benefit from you posting about them and vice versa.

## STAY ON BRAND

Keep photos similar to your style and on brand by keeping them simple and clean. Have a theme that runs through your posts, whether it be a certain crop that you use or a coloured object in each post – you want people to have a reason to visit your page again and again.

## KEEP CAPTIONS SHORT AND SHARP

Humorous captions usually work best, but keep them short and sweet.

# HOW TO MASTER THE FLAT LAY

*You might be wondering what you're actually going to include in your Instagram posts! Well look no further – the most innovative and fun (albeit time-consuming) way to get your brand message across is by creating a flat lay – a composed collage that looks like you've just scattered your favourite objects on the floor/desk/rug and taken a photo of them from above so they look 'flat' (have a look at the posts with the hashtag #flatlay for a better idea). These types of posts have become increasingly popular and can be shared, posted by other Instagrammers and used as banners for your business website as well. Doing a good flat lay is no mean feat. Here are our top tips to getting that perfect square.*

## YOUR HERO ITEM

The reason for posting a flat lay is usually to highlight one specific object and to make it look as appealing as possible. If you are selling a candle or lipstick, a new book, flower business – whatever it is, make sure you have one readily available and in good condition to photograph. Then start collecting objects in a similar colour scheme. If your object is pale blue, pick objects in pastel hues. If your product is white or black, opt for a monochrome palette with one item that has a pop of colour. Look for things around the house – for example candles, sunglasses, a pen, notebook, perfume bottle, jewellery, a cup of tea, a laptop, strawberries ... Because when put together correctly, everyday objects can look extraordinary in a flat lay.

## GOOD LIGHTING

Next, find the spot in your house or office that has the best source of natural light. It is advisable to use a good quality camera, but no matter how good your equipment is, natural light will always beat out newfangled cameras and technical photo-editing apps.

## BACKGROUND

Flat lays look best on a neutral background. Art shops are a treasure trove of good backdrops – a simple piece of white cardboard, a marbled piece of paper, a marble bench top, a grey floor board, a gorgeous desk, an outdoor dining table, a beautiful rug – the choices are endless. White, though, will always help your flat lay pop. Try a white table, desk, coffee table book or even a white bed sheet.

## THE LAYOUT

Some of the high profile influencers swear by the rule of six – and split the screen up into an invisible grid of six smaller squares, placing an object in each. Don't think that each object needs to face forwards either – having everything on an angle creates an engaging flat lay. Make sure to leave space around your objects so your photo doesn't look too cluttered.

ON THE ROCKS

PHOTOGRAPHY DANIEL JACKSON
STYLING MATTIAS KARLSSON

VOGUE

CHANEL
CHANEL COLLECTIONS AND CREATIONS
In VOGUE
TOM FORD

THE GAME CHANGERS
SUCCESS SECRETS FROM 40 WOMEN AT THE TOP

## THE BIRD'S-EYE VIEW

Stand on a stool so that you can take the best shot of your flat lay. If you're using an iPhone, take the photo in a 'square' so you don't have to crop your photo later.

## EDITING

Less editing is always best, but with the myriad of apps available at your disposal, you can always improve the quality of your image. You can adjust the contrast and lighting to make the image appear crisper and put a filter on it to make it look more professional, helping your images to stand out. Our favourite apps for editing flat lays include Snapseed, for playing around with the clarity, sharpness, contrast, shadows and ambiance; VSCO, which has a number of different filters that you can play around with; and Facetune, to brighten your background and to make your objects sharper and clearer with the sharpening tool.

## TAGGING

Like any Instagram post, tagging is key to getting your flat lay image noticed. Make sure to tag all the brands you have used in your photo as often brands will regram to help you gain an organic following.

## PLAN YOUR GRAM

A brilliant app to use is Plann, which helps you plan your Instagram posts ahead of time. That way you can see if your previous post matches your next post and how your flat lays look on your Instagram page amongst your other photos. You can tweak your content or filter to match the previous posts. You want to create a running theme for your top six squares.

# THE GAME CHANGING RULES OF STYLE

*If you have a good blow dry, manicured nails and a spray tan you don't have to splurge on expensive clothes, shoes or handbags. Having style isn't always about the dollar value of your wears or how many designer items you own. Even the most extravagant fashionistas will attest that it's about a good fit, a beautiful fabric, a great hemline, a pop of colour. It's about feeling confident in your own skin and wearing your outfit with self-assurance and conviction. But while style can't always be bought, if you have to buy just one thing to add to your wardrobe, here is our short list.*

**THE CLASSIC HANDBAG**
Forget what's trending or high street style. The Game Changing women we polled often invested in one classic handbag (when they could afford it!). Pick pieces that will last the distance, from the timeless classics such as Chanel or Dior. These bags will last you for decades and will still look as good due to their quality materials, not to mention make any outfit look a million dollars.

**THE INVESTMENT COAT/JACKET**
One beautiful coat will update any look while jet-setting around the globe or for that all-important job interview. It can dress up a great pair of jeans or be thrown over a slick suit or a cocktail dress. Opt for a good quality thick fabric in a muted colour or simple black that can be worn every winter for years to come.

**A FABULOUS SHOE**
A beautiful designer shoe or strappy heel will also last the distance and enhance any outfit. After all, high heels do something wonderful to a woman's legs and butt, without her ever having to do any squats or lunges.

**THE COCKTAIL DRESS**
The good news is you need just one elegant, long cocktail dress that you can bring out of the closet for a work function, charity ball, relative's wedding or Christmas party without feeling overwhelmed that you have with nothing to wear or no budget to buy something when an invite lands in your letter box at the last minute. Invest in something that makes you feel amazing and have it tailored to fit your body shape. Alternatively, there are a number of last minute dress hire websites that have recently popped up that allow you to borrow a designer dress for a few days at a fraction of the cost. Try glamcorner.com.au which is our go-to for designer in season frocks.

## THE CASHMERE PIECE

A cashmere cardigan or wrap is the perfect luxury piece that will last for years to come. It will update every wardrobe and is perfect to throw over everything. It can dress up the most casual of outfits for dinners, travelling on planes and in the height of the winter months.

## NEVER BUY ACCORDING TO TRENDS WHEN SPENDING BIG

We have all made the mistake of buying a trendy designer piece only to wear it once while it breaks the bank account! When buying designer pieces, opt for classics that will go with everything and that you can wear time and time again. Stick to items that suit your shape and can be dressed up or dressed down depending on your occasion. And don't be afraid to mix and match high style with more affordable items; a basic white t-shirt can go a long way when teamed with the right accessories.

## BEST WEBSITES TO BUY FROM

### For second hand luxury:

Make sure to check out any second hand shops, you can always find a bargain. Also you can hit up these websites: www.c21stores.com; www.therealreal.com; www.portero.com; www.fashionphile.com; www.theoutnet.com; www.deuxieme.co.uk.

### For those with bigger budgets:

www.net-a-porter.com; www.mytheresa.com; www.selfridges.com; www.neimanmarcus.com; www.shoprachelzoe.com; www.melissaodabash.com; www.stylerunner.com; www.davidjones.com.au; www.myer.com.au.

### For borrowing items:

www.glamcorner.com.au; www.mydressaffair.com.au; www.theluxecollectionbyl.com.au.

# OUR TOP
## GAME CHANGING
# *BEAUTY*
# PRODUCTS 6

### LA PRAIRIE SKIN CAVIAR LUXE SLEEP MASK, LUXE CREAM AND LIQUID LIFT
This combination of a luxurious mask, serum and moisturiser is the Game Changing combination that every girl needs. La Prairie will change your skin overnight leaving it soft, supple and hydrated.

### HOURGLASS LIGHT CORRECTING PRIMER
Makeup artists say it's a crime not to prime your skin before you begin your makeup. Think of it like greasing the pan before you cook a steak. We love this lightweight version by Hourglass. It's oil free, airy and hides redness, pores and even wrinkles. (Mecca Cosmetica)

### EVE LOM CLEANSER
This not only removes all traces of the day from your face (including heavy makeup) but gives you a light exfoliation as well. It will close your pores and leave you feeling fresh and glowy. (Mecca Cosmetica)

### DR DENNIS GROSS HYALURONIC MARINE HYDRATING MODELING MASK
When your skin is looking dry and dull, skin gurus swear by this two-step mask to give you dewy, radiating skin and hydration in just five minutes. (Mecca Cosmetica)

### CHANEL GARDENIA
If you have to pick one fragrance, try Chanel's Gardenia – a delicious floral bouquet created by the great perfumer Ernest Beaux in 1925. It was relaunched in the 1980s, but still encompasses its original timeless elegance. Spritz on for everyday glamour.

### DIPTYQUE CANDLES
When it comes to Game Changing beauty products, you can't go past the legendary French brand Diptyque for their luxurious look and distinctive olfactory signatures that delight the senses, instantly changing the dynamic of any home: the ultimate style statement. Our favourites are Baies, Tubereuse and Figuier. (Mecca Cosmetica)

# OUR TOP
## GAME CHANGING
# *MAKEUP*
## PRODUCTS 12

### NARS CREAMY CONCEALER

Got a zit? Bags under your eyes? This concealer is a lifesaver when it comes to hiding any imperfections. Think of it as an eraser button for your face. No one will ever know what was underneath.

### GLINDAWAND COSMETICA CHEEK COLOUR IN OPHELIA

This handmade blush, created by television and celebrity makeup artist Jacqui Hutton, contains flecks of gold dust, giving your face that back-from-St-Barts glow. Each powder is made from mixed liquid pigments baked in individual terracotta pans.

### BECCA SHIMMERING SKIN PERFECTOR PRESSED HIGHLIGHTER IN MOONSTONE

This genius product acts like a 'spotlight for your skin', giving you a radiant, shimmering glow without being cakey.

### KEVYN AUCOIN CELESTIAL SKIN LIQUID LIGHTING

Makeup artists just love this secret weapon. We love to mix this into our foundation for luminous, glowing skin.

### BOBBI BROWN BRONZE SHIMMER BRICK

This creates a deep bronze glow without looking too heavy or giving those stripy 'bronzed' lines.

### CHARLOTTE TILBURY LIPSTICK IN RED CARPET

Celebrities are obsessed with Charlotte Tilbury lipsticks beause of their long-lasting power and no-bleed promise and we agree. Red Carpet Red is our go-to colour to glam up everyday outfits or for transforming day to night with one quick swipe.

## LANCÔME HYPNÔSE MASCARA

We love false eyelashes for special occasions but for the everyday, nothing beats the classic Lancôme mascara. This one is spiked with vitamin B, it's smudge-resistant and will last for hours without pulling out your lashes.

## HOURGLASS VEIL MINERAL PRIMER

Makeup artists say it's a crime not to prime your skin before you begin your makeup. Think of it like greasing the pan before you cook a steak. We love this lightweight version by Hourglass. It's oil free, airy and hides redness, pores and even wrinkles.

## ELLIS FAAS SKIN VEIL FOUNDATION

We love this creamy, glossy, glowing light-coverage foundation. It literally creates a veil over your skin and if you get the colour professionally matched to your skin tone, it will blend flawlessly into every complexion.

## TOM FORD EYE DEFINING PEN

If you wear nothing else, it should be a winged liner across your upper lid for that everyday no-makeup-yet-oh-so-polished look. We love Tom Ford's easy-to-use pen, which opens up your eyes without the need for much else.

## BEAUTY BLENDER FOUNDATION SPONGE

Nothing looks good if it ain't blended! Which is why this Beauty Blender sponge is a staple in every in-the-know gal's handbag. Blend, blend, blend for that photo finish.

## MAC STUDIO FIX POWDER PLUS FOUNDATION

The ultimate when it comes to the perfect powder over your foundation. It will help keep makeup on all day and night – the perfect beauty fix.

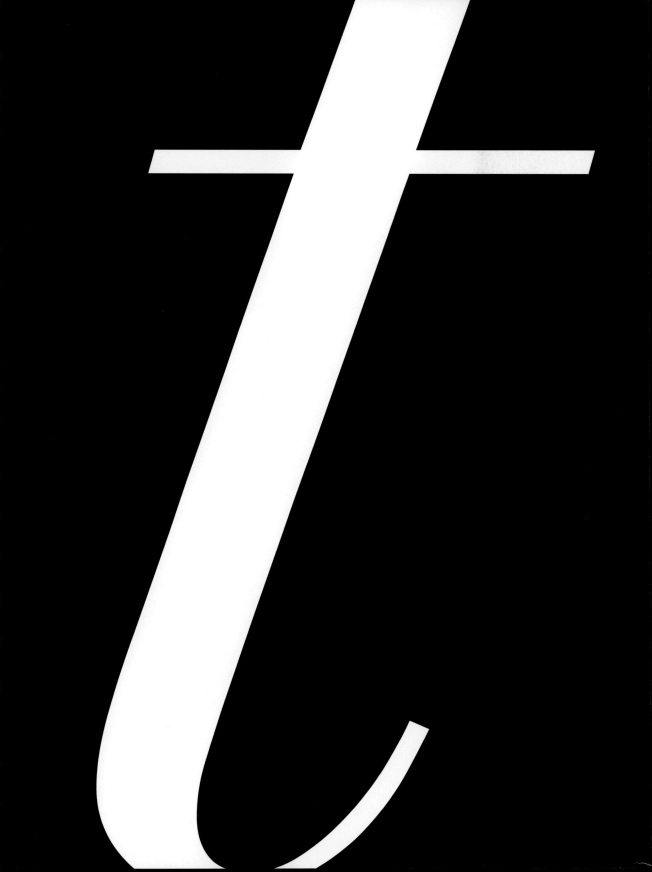

# the GAME CHANGERS

# ARIANNA HUFFINGTON

CO-FOUNDER OF *THE HUFFINGTON POST*, AUTHOR,
FOUNDER AND CEO OF THRIVE GLOBAL

*Named as one of the world's most powerful women by* Forbes *magazine, Arianna Huffington is a true trailblazer. After launching the news and blog website* The Huffington Post *in 2005, the site was acquired by AOL in 2011 for more than $300 million and won the prestigious Pulitzer Prize in 2012. Arianna is the author of fifteen books and continues to be one of the most inspiring, Game Changing women on the planet. She is the founder and CEO of Thrive Global, a corporate and consumer wellbeing and productivity platform aimed at changing the way we work and live.*

In college, I joined the Cambridge Union debate society. A British publisher, who had published Germaine Greer's *The Female Eunuch*, happened to see me on television debating the importance of women not throwing the baby out with the bathwater, so to speak. The publisher sent me a letter asking if I would be interested in writing a book on my views.

I was in my last year at Cambridge and was planning to leave the next year to get a graduate degree at the Kennedy School of Government at Harvard. So, I sent him a letter saying, 'Thank you, but I don't know how to write a book.' He wrote back: 'Can you have lunch?'

Thinking of all my friends wandering around looking for a home for their manuscript, I decided it was at least worth a train ride to London. By the end of lunch, Reg Davis-Poynter had offered me a contract and a modest advance. That contract marked a new beginning in my life, setting me on a path – though I didn't know it at the time – to writing more books and, many years later, co-founding *The Huffington Post*. My second book was rejected by

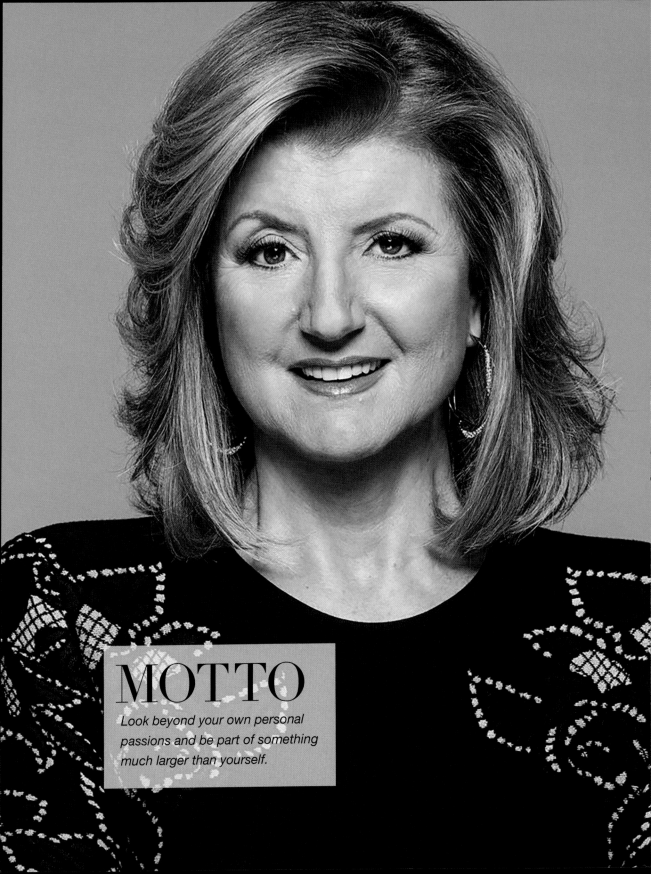

## MOTTO

*Look beyond your own personal passions and be part of something much larger than yourself.*

thirty-seven publishers. By about rejection twenty-five, you would have thought I might have said, 'Hey, you know, there's something wrong here. Maybe I should be looking at a different career.' Instead, I remember running out of money and walking, depressed, down St. James Street in London and seeing a Barclays Bank. I walked in and, armed with nothing but a lot of chutzpah, I asked to speak to the manager and asked him for a loan. Even though I didn't have any assets, the banker – whose name was Ian Bell – gave me a loan. It changed my life, because it meant I could keep things together for another thirteen rejections.

And then I got an acceptance. In fairytales, there are helpful animals that come out of nowhere to help the hero or heroine through a dark and difficult time, often helping them find a way out of the forest. Well, in life too, there are helpful animals disguised as human beings – like Ian Bell, to whom I still send a Christmas card every year. So, very often, the difference between success and failure is perseverance. It's how long we can keep going until success happens. It's getting up one more time than we fall down.

In 2003, I ran for governor of California, part of a large field of candidates that included the ultimate victor, Arnold Schwarzenegger. As exhilarating

## Arianna's *TIPS*

- Experiment and take risks.

- Remember to look beyond your own personal passions and be part of something larger than yourself.

- Sleep ranks number one! How much sleep we have will determine, in no small measure, our ability to address and solve the problems we're facing as individuals and as a society.

as the experience was, it also had its bruising moments. Schwarzenegger expressed his displeasure at having to debate a full-throttle female by suggesting that I drink more decaf – a comment that is hard to imagine being addressed to a man. In fact, that debate made me realise how deeply ingrained our culture's fear of assertive women is and how much of this fear women have unconsciously internalised. After the debate, I came off the stage and was immediately surrounded by dozens of young female students who thanked me for taking a stand and not backing down.

## THE HUFFINGTON POST

Bringing together people from different parts of my life and facilitating interesting conversations has always been part of my Greek DNA. So from the beginning, the whole point of *The Huffington Post* was to take the sort of conversations found at water coolers and around dinner tables – about politics, art, books, food and sex – and open them up and bring them online.

When we launched *The Huffington Post* in 2005, it received decidedly mixed reviews, including one that said the site was 'the movie equivalent of *Gigli*, *Ishtar* and *Heaven's Gate* rolled into one.' And a year later, when that same reviewer emailed me to ask about blogging for *The Huffington Post*, I happily said yes, since holding grudges is one of the most draining things you can do. Back then, many people – including some of the most powerful and influential people in the world of media – still regarded blogging as something different and distinctly less than the familiar modes of op-eds and storytelling. Eleven years later, no one is making that argument – at least no one who is interested in using all the tools at our disposal to tell the stories of our time.

Sam Stein was our first reporter, and I often fondly reminisce about our humble beginnings. Our first DC office was actually one room that we got for free (we couldn't afford rent yet) after I called David Bradley, the publisher of *The Atlantic*, and begged for some free space in one of his buildings that was in the process of being renovated. Now, we have editions in sixteen countries, with more than 850 editors and reporters around the world, with half our traffic coming from outside the US.

## THRIVE GLOBAL

Since publishing my books *Thrive* and then *The Sleep Revolution*, I've dreamed of taking the next big step to help transform the way we work and live. When I decided to create Thrive Global, I thought it would be possible to build a start-up and continue as editor in chief of *The Huffington Post*. But as Thrive Global moved from an idea to a reality, with investors, staff, and offices, it became clear to me that I simply couldn't do justice to both companies. Change is desperately needed if another generation is to avoid the burnout that all too often comes with success today. That's why I'm filled with excitement at the prospect of devoting the rest of my life to accelerating the culture shift away from merely surviving and succeeding to thriving.

To truly thrive means knowing when the time has come to close one chapter and start the next.

# JULIE BISHOP

AUSTRALIAN MINISTER FOR FOREIGN AFFAIRS,
DEPUTY LEADER OF THE LIBERAL PARTY

*A true trailblazer for women in politics and law, Julie Bishop is Australia's top diplomat and is presently one of four female members of Cabinet in Australia. Through her work as Foreign Minister since 2013, she has cemented her position on the world stage through her tireless work with victims of the MH17 tragedy and raising awareness about refugee women in the Middle East. The Minister was named Woman of The Year by* Harper's Bazaar *in 2014.*

Before I entered politics, I was the managing partner in Perth of a national law firm, and was a board member of a number of business and community organisations. I was admitted to practise law in South Australia, New South Wales, Western Australia and in the High Court. My main area of practice was in commercial litigation, but I also specialised in defamation law. I handled a wide variety of challenging cases over a 20 year career in the law.

In 1996 I took a sabbatical from Clayton Utz law firm to complete the Advanced Management Program for Senior Managers at Harvard Business School, and during my time away I considered a career change. Given my interest in foreign affairs, public policy and community service, I believed I could make a contribution to national politics. I returned to Australia after completing the Advanced Management Program at Harvard in 1996. Two years later I was endorsed as the Liberal candidate for the electorate of Curtin and won that seat in the October 1998 Federal Election. I have now been the Federal Member for Curtin for almost nineteen years. Before that I had been involved in the Liberal Party in Perth and held party positions including as a branch President. My family are lifelong Liberal supporters, my mother was involved in local government in South Australia, including as the local mayor, so I was familiar with and exposed to politics from a young age. My biggest challenge at this time was winning the seat of Curtin from an Independent who had been the local member for many years.

## MOTTO

*Trust my instincts, back my judgment, and don't let others define me.*

## AUSTRALIA'S FIRST FEMALE DEPUTY LEADER

There are two positions in the parliamentary Liberal Party that are directly elected by the Party Room – Leader and Deputy Leader. I was honoured to be elected Deputy Leader by my colleagues in 2007 and I see it as my duty to represent the interests of our members and senators. I have been re-elected to this position on a number of occasions over the past ten years, and I am the first woman to hold the position.

## BECOMING FOREIGN MINISTER

My interest in Australia's place in the world was enhanced during my first overseas trip as a university student and later through my work with regional and global legal networks. On entering Parliament, I chaired the Government's Policy Committee on Foreign Affairs, and later the Joint Standing Committee on Treaties, furthering my interest in foreign affairs.

I was sworn in as Australia's first female Foreign Minister in 2013. It is a privilege to serve in this position and represent Australia's interests and priorities on the world stage.

I am very proud of the New Colombo Plan, a landmark initiative I established in 2013. By the end of 2017, almost 18 000 undergraduates from Australian universities will have completed part of their studies under this program; living, studying and undertaking work experience in one of forty locations in the Indo-Pacific. This initiative has the capacity to transform the lives of the students, as well as ensure that Australia's deep engagement in the region endures for generations.

The innovationXchange is another policy initiative I believe will transform public policy, embracing new and creative ways to deliver overseas development assistance (aid) in the Indo-Pacific.

Presiding over the United Nations Security Council and securing a unanimous resolution to gain access to the MH17 Malaysian Airlines crash zone in Ukraine, and engaging with the families of those killed on that flight, was a significant challenge.

The growing ambitions of rising powers, an uncertain political landscape in parts of Europe, heightened geopolitical risks, global terrorism, the impact of digital disruption, the slowdown in global trade and uneven trends in the global economy are some of the challenges I deal with as Foreign Minister, as well as managing our bilateral relationships with countries around the globe.

**WORKING ALONGSIDE AMAL CLOONEY TO SEEK JUSTICE FOR FEMALE VICTIMS OF ISIS**

I am gravely concerned about the plight of the Yazidis and have met with Nadia Murad, a young Yazidi who is now an active advocate around the world for their cause, and with Amal Clooney who acts as Counsel for the Yazidis. Together we have participated in meetings at the United Nations General Assembly, including 'Bringing Daesh to Justice' meeting last September. Amal is a delightful person and an intelligent and passionate human rights advocate.

Australia has long condemned the appalling abuses committed by ISIS/Daesh including against the Yazidis. We strongly advocate holding individual terrorists to account for their terrible crimes. Yazidi women have been subjected to atrocities and we are committed to seeking justice for them and other victims of ISIS.

**FLIGHT MH17**

In July 2014 the world was horrified by reports that a commercial airliner carrying 298 innocent passengers and crew had been shot down over Eastern Ukraine. Australia moved swiftly to bring an internationally backed resolution for an open, thorough and impartial investigation to find out who perpetrated this act. We were able to secure a unanimous Security Council resolution providing full access to the Malaysia Airlines flight MH17 crash site in Eastern Ukraine. I also negotiated with the Ukraine Government to enable Australian law enforcement and investigation teams to access the crash site – this involved convincing the Ukraine Government to recall its Parliament during the summer break to pass necessary legislation.

Later that year, I was awarded a Commander of the Order of Merit from the Netherlands Ministry of Foreign Affairs for our efforts to achieve justice for the victims and their loved ones.

**HITCHING A RIDE ON AIR FORCE 3 WITH JOHN KERRY**

Both Secretary Kerry and I were in Myanmar for the East Asia Summit, and I was to host him in Sydney the following day for our annual Australia–US ministerial meeting. There were no commercial flights that would get me back to Australia in time so the answer seemed obvious – catch a lift with Secretary Kerry on his US Airforce plane. On landing in Australia, I ran down the stairs first, so I was on the tarmac to greet him when he descended the stairs.

## A CHAMPION OF WOMEN

I have always sought to focus on the opportunities for women and girls, rather than the obstacles to their advancement. There are many examples of conscious and unconscious bias against women but many women provide inspirational examples of how to overcome it.

Throughout my professional career, I have held a strong belief that women should empower other women, whether through formal or informal mentoring, or simply by supporting each other as colleagues in the work place. I encourage women to consider a career in politics, but I am mindful of the fact that it is not a career everyone would want to pursue.

I think there is definitely room for more female leaders in the world. Women make up about half the population. Empowering women is one of the most effective ways to promote peace, prosperity and human rights. I have introduced programs to support emerging women leaders in the Pacific.

I have found my career as a woman in politics to be rewarding and satisfying, more of a vocation than a career. My advice to women wanting to enter politics is that the public scrutiny can be intense, but if you believe entering public office is one of the highest callings, then entering politics gives you the opportunity to contribute to the betterment of your community and nation.

# DREAMING AFTER ALL, IS A FORM OF PLANNING

GLORIA STEINEM

# RACHEL ZOE

FASHION DESIGNER, STYLIST, BUSINESSWOMAN

*The doyenne of fearlessness, Rachel Zoe is a fashion designer, stylist and businesswoman. She is best known for dressing some the world's most celebrated women in her signature effortless, glamorous style.*

P rior to the journey of my career, I was a student at George Washington University majoring in sociology and psychology. Growing up, I didn't know what a stylist was, but I was obsessed with fashion magazines and inspired by the images they conveyed and the stories they told. I knew I needed to be part of the process, the execution – how it all came to fruition. My idol from a very young age was Grace Coddington. She is someone I will always look up to. She is a true artist of fashion.

In my early 20s, I worked as a fashion editor at *YM* magazine. It was an incredibly valuable experience and I was so in love with it. After my first day, I knew this was what I was meant to do.

My first big break came in 1998, when Tommy Hilfiger hired me to style one of his major ad campaigns – the iconic White House campaign, which was a huge production. We worked for two weeks in Los Angeles and Austin. It was by far my biggest job yet. Knowing that someone like Tommy believed in me at that point in my career was incredibly encouraging. My client roster began to grow, from musicians of the moment (Britney Spears, Enrique Iglesias, the Backstreet Boys, Jessica Simpson) to Cameron Diaz, Kate Hudson and Salma Hayek. I absolutely loved styling. I worked twenty-four hours a day, was constantly on an aeroplane and lived for every second of it!

## FROM STYLIST
## TO BUSINESSWOMAN

The transition from stylist to businesswoman happened very naturally and organically. Joining forces with my husband, Rodger, who was a longtime investment banker and entrepreneur, made the transition feel seamless. Our challenge, even today, is learning how to manage the growth of the brand, to find the right balance between small-business culture and corporate structure. The business took off quickly and we knew we had to ramp up our infrastructure with an incredible team. I went from working with a few assistants to hiring more than fifty employees in just a few years. One of the biggest accomplishments of my career was my first collection, which launched in the fall of 2011 when I was nine months pregnant with my first son, Skyler. It was unquestionably one of my proudest moments.

I owe so much of my success to those who have supported me, especially my parents, who've inspired and guided me along my career path. My dad is a self-made entrepreneur who showed me it's possible to succeed while still being kind and maintaining a sense of integrity. My mother taught me to live life glamorously. In business, fearless leaders like Diane Von Furstenberg, Marc Jacobs, Stella McCartney, Tommy Hilfiger and my own clients have guided me in different aspects of my career. I owe them everything.

# Rachel's
# TIPS

- Do not feel entitled! Success doesn't just happen to you.

- You can be successful and kind. You don't have to step on people to get where you need to be. Be honest and loyal, and you will win.

- Don't be intimidated by what seems to be a man's world – we know more and can do it better, generally speaking.

- Always show what you're made of – don't hold back. You add value to any situation.

- It doesn't get easier – it gets better. Work towards your goals the old-school way, with hard work and dedication.

- Don't expect a pat on the back for everything you do. When working up, your job can be thankless, but don't lose steam!

My successes can also be attributed to my passion for what I do. My career is driven by my genuine love of fashion and the transformative power of style. In the beginning, I was motivated by my desire to be the best at my job. To this day, I put 100 per cent into everything I do. I never take no for an answer. And I cannot stress how important it is to be adaptive and flexible. I continue to learn new things every day. You must embrace change, though it's often hard to do.

I make it a point to drive my business with integrity – I think consumers can sense authenticity and can tell when a message isn't genuine. I've always been driven by passion, not by money, and I've never looked at my job as work but as a way of life. I am so grateful that I love going to work every day, and I never take that for granted.

Of course there have been setbacks. One of my biggest challenges is knowing when to trust people. Getting hurt by those I'm close to is hard for me, but you have to take the high road and move on, and it makes you stronger in the end.

**THE ZOE CLIENTELE**

All my clients have been so exciting to work with, both personally and professionally. Some notables include Keira Knightley, Salma Hayek, Jennifer Lawrence, Jennifer Garner, Anne Hathaway, Kate Hudson, Eva Mendes and Cameron Diaz. I've been so fortunate to have an extraordinary connectivity with my clients, both creatively and emotionally. I've remained close friends with many of them, and our mutual support of one another's endeavors is amazing.

**THE RACHEL ZOE BRAND**

I like to think of my brand as both inspirational and aspirational, empowering women through living a life in style. My collection is designed for both the trendy and the traditional, the modern and the classic. It's fashionable and functional, befitting a range of lifestyles, ages and occasions.

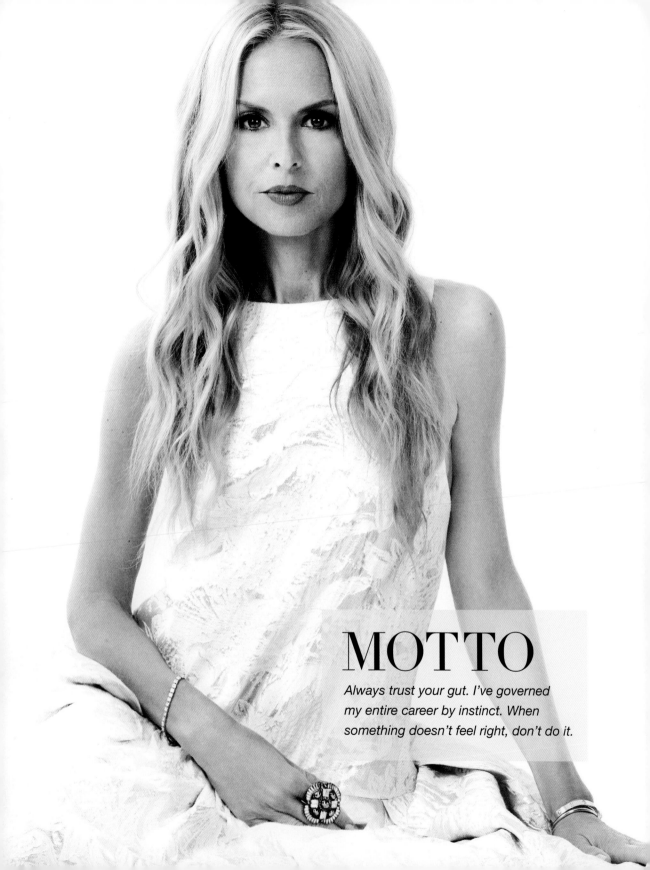

# MOTTO

*Always trust your gut. I've governed
my entire career by instinct. When
something doesn't feel right, don't do it.*

**GETTING THE MESSAGE OUT**

I started The Zoe Report more than seven years ago as a way to connect with style-obsessed women. Since then, my team and I have been devoted to creating useful, inspiring content for our growing audience. It's proven to be a very important channel for establishing an authentic dialogue with my readers, and social media has become a huge part of how we amplify the content we publish.

From a product standpoint, building relationships with customers via our luxury subscription service Box of Style and through our ecommerce site RachelZoe.com has been amazing.

These digital platforms are instrumental in providing access to my brand – they help me understand instantly what my audience is wanting right now and they allow my team and me to react quickly. A big part of our company's mission is harnessing customer feedback in order to expand and improve on our products and experiences.

# MOTTO

*Jump and the net will appear.*

# ELLE MACPHERSON

BUSINESSWOMAN, SUPERMODEL, MOTHER,
CO-FOUNDER OF WELLECO

*Elle Macpherson is an Australian model, businesswoman and TV presenter. She has carved out a diverse career over the past thirty years, starting with her early modelling career, which led to a record-breaking five* Sports Illustrated *covers, affording her global recognition and the nickname 'The Body' from* Time *magazine. She is the founder and co-owner of her lingerie brand Elle Macpherson Body. In 2014, she co-founded WelleCo, and released its flagship product The Super Elixir. She is currently the European Ambassador for RED, raising money for the global fund to fight HIV/AIDS in Africa. She works closely with The Women's Fund focusing on women's issues and empowerment in her new hometown, Miami, and has a longstanding connection to The National Association for Children of Alcoholics in the UK.*

## THE ACCIDENTAL EXECUTIVE

I realised early on in my career that it would be best if I could create content and produce my own independent material. I left traditional model agencies to form my own company, Elle Macpherson Inc, when I was twenty-five years old. I partnered with a fantastic business manager who helped teach me to be the creator of my career. From there, I licensed my name in various categories, built a strong thirty year lingerie business, produced swimsuit calendars and created content for network TV. I started to produce and host various TV shows (as the Executive Producer), including *Fashion Star* for NBC and *Britain's Next Top Model*. Today my business strategies have evolved and I am a passionate co-founder and co-owner of wellness company WelleCo and I co-own a 50/50 joint venture of Elle Macpherson Body.

## THE EVOLUTION OF THE SUPER ELIXIR

I discovered the profound benefit of good nutrition and living alkaline from my nutritional doctor, Dr Simone Laubscher, and I wanted to share it. The most important thing to me is how I feel and I've found that if my body is getting the nutrients it needs then it shows on the outside – beauty fom the inside out.

I teamed up with Andrea Horwood Bux (another Aussie and founder of Invisible Zinc whose inspiring personal story you can also read in this book) to form WelleCo. We knew there would be easier products to start with, but our Super Elixir Alkalising Greens are the core of WelleCo and why we exist, so we began with that. We tested the product for years, changing and modifying to develop the perfect formula. Yes, it took time to communicate properly, but our customers started doing the talking for us. The more people who discovered and started taking The Super Elixir, the more they wanted to share it. It grew organically, you could say.

It's been a fast trajectory upwards ever since, with a huge growth in staff and wellness products that we now offer. Nourishing Protein, Sleep Welle Calming Tea, Kids Nourishing Protein and a wonderful Alkalising Greens gold caddy collaboration with Aerin Lauder.

I attribute its success to it being a great, quality product and an honest story. It's easily accessible, delivered to your doorstep and it works!

## CAREER LONGEVITY

Love, laughter and water! I believe in courage, co-operation, perseverance, passion and being the creator of your own life – I've found if you do what you love and love what you do – the by-product is success!

# *Elle's*
# ADVICE

- Find co-dreamers: people who understand and support your dreams.

- Visualise exactly what you want to create in detail.

- Write, collect images and make mood boards.

- Share dreams and watch them grow.

- Appreciate all the baby steps it takes to make a leap forward.

*PEOPLE RESPOND WELL TO PEOPLE WHO ARE SURE OF WHAT THEY WANT*

ANNA WINTOUR

# GWYNETH PALTROW

ACADEMY AWARD–WINNING ACTRESS, ENTREPRENEUR, FOUNDER
OF GOOP, CREATIVE DIRECTOR OF JUICE BEAUTY MAKEUP

*From acting, to writing cookbooks, to ecommerce, Gwyneth Paltrow is open to sharing her lifestyle with the world. She has turned her musings into a successful multi-million dollar brand. The Oscar-winning actress established an online presence with her start-up Goop in 2008, and the brand continues to push boundaries, gain momentum and build into a force to be reckoned with. Many were quick to dismiss her foray into ecommerce, but as she told the* New York Times, *'There's a lot of resistance to women coming to the table with anything new. But if it were Justin Timberlake or Jay Z or even Donald Trump, everyone would be okay with it.'*

My life started to get interesting after I turned forty. I think it's the strange irony that we make all these life choices before we're forty, because really we shouldn't make any until we're forty. It almost feels like you get a software upgrade and you start to experience life in such a different way, because you just don't suffer fools, you go straight for what means something and what feels good, and you stop caring about pleasing other people. I thought maybe I could give my daughter this wisdom so she doesn't waste all that time like I did, but the process is the process.

*NEVER DOUBT THAT YOU ARE VALUABLE AND POWERFUL AND DESERVING OF EVERY CHANCE IN THE WORLD TO PURSUE YOUR DREAMS*

**HILLARY CLINTON**

## MOTTO

*One woman can change anything.*
*Many women can change everything.*

# LAURIE ADAMS

PRESIDENT OF WOMEN FOR WOMEN INTERNATIONAL

*Laurie Adams is a true champion of women, dedicating her life to helping others. She is the President of Women For Women International, which focuses on empowering female survivors of war. The organisation has served almost half a million women who've survived wars in Afghanistan, Bosnia and Herzegovina, the Democratic Republic of the Congo, Iraq, Kosovo, Nigeria, Rwanda and South Sudan.*

My personal and professional life has been global. I was born in Korea and raised in Germany and Italy. I went to school in the United States, Hungary, and Nicaragua and have lived my adult life in Senegal, Kenya, the United Kingdom, and South Africa. I've had the chance to work with global organisations like ActionAid International as well as found and organise local grassroots efforts such as The Other Foundation, which focuses on equality, gender, and sexual orientation in southern Africa. Before joining Women for Women International, I was the Director of Women's Rights for Oxfam in the United Kingdom and managed programs in several African countries.

My university degree was in Government with a minor in Education and certificate in Gender Studies, but my real learning took place outside the classroom. I was very active in student movements to end racism and sexism on campus – including to get Dartmouth to divest from the apartheid government in South Africa. I learned how to negotiate with power holders such as trustees and the administration, how to speak publicly and how to write and edit, and make my voice heard. I also learned desktop publishing, fundraising, and organising while working on campus and in South Africa to end apartheid and advance equality.

## CHANGING SOUTH AFRICA

Growing up with a black sister, I witnessed racism in a personal way. It made me see that racism isn't an issue that impacts nameless strangers, but one that impacts my own family. This led me to join the anti-apartheid movement and devote my life to it. When Nelson Mandela was released in 1990, I was given the incredible opportunity to move to South Africa and represent two US organisations. I leaped at the chance to help build a new democratic South Africa and the decision changed my life.

I did a wide range of work in South Africa. I started out working with US organisations and then had the opportunity to work with local institutions. Later, I worked with global organisations and I had the chance to live, visit, and work in more than twenty African countries. I have had the great privilege of spending months discussing gender roles amongst nomadic people in places like Kenya and Mali, being at the bargaining table deciding trade rules with Ministers and even Presidents, and being a first responder, saving lives from conflict and natural disasters ranging from Liberia to Angola. South Africa was a fantastic start to a life full of adventure, growth and learning for me.

## WOMEN FOR WOMEN INTERNATIONAL

Women for Women International (WfWI) is a grassroots organisation committed to long-term and sustainable investment in the empowerment of women survivors of war around the world. We work with the most marginalised and socially-excluded women so they have the skills, networks, and tools they need to rebuild their lives, communities, and nations. Through our comprehensive 12 month program, women learn about their rights and health, and gain key life, vocational, and business skills to access livelihoods and break free from trauma and poverty. We have served more than 462 000 women survivors of war in Afghanistan, Bosnia and Herzegovina, the Democratic Republic of the Congo, Iraq, Kosovo, Nigeria, Rwanda, and South Sudan.

What I love about WfWI's work is its comprehensive nature. We don't work only on economic empowerment, or only on health – we work with women as whole human beings with many facets to their lives. Our program helps women become economically empowered, but we also provide information about health and wellbeing and family planning. We also make it possible for women to create savings groups and support systems and teach women about their rights and the value of their lives and their work. In addition, we work with men.

Through our work, we've learned that when men are engaged as allies in the fight for equality in their communities, they bring in more men and create a ripple effect of change.

This is why we ensure that the men we work with know about women's rights and the value of women's lives and work as well. We've reached more than 15 000 men through our men's engagement program.

## EXPANDING THE REACH

Even after twenty-five years of work, everywhere we go we see high demand for our program. Recently, during our leadership team's visit to Nigeria, we noticed that on enrolment day, hundreds of women were standing at a church parking lot to sign up for our training. The program had reached its limit for new enrolments and the women were told that the classes were full and they should go home. They didn't. Rather they came back the next day, and the day after, and the day after that hoping a spot would open for them. At WfWI, we are always thinking about how we can expand our work. We want to reach women where they are. Right now, we are opening a country office in Erbil in Northern Iraq and exploring opening an office in Jordan to serve more Syrian and Iraqi refugees. We are also finding partners to work with in South Sudan, where famine and unrest is threatening the lives of many and has displaced 3.5 million people.

As we look to the future, we are aiming for a day when we will not have to turn away another woman. We hope one day we will have the capacity to accept every single woman in that church parking lot.

## SUPPORTING SYRIAN AND YEZIDI SURVIVORS OF WAR AND GENOCIDE

We see time and time again that during modern conflicts women's bodies are used as battlefields and rape is a weapon to silence and marginalise women and tear apart communities. In Iraq and Syria, ISIS has abducted thousands of women, sold them in marketplaces like commodities, and turned them into sexual slaves. Even after freedom from ISIS, women live with an immense amount of trauma: the fabric of their communities and families is broken, and they are left without any support systems. In addition to the overt physical violence against and sexual exploitation of women committed by ISIS, millions of women and their families have been displaced or become refugees due to the conflict.

Women continue to face violence and abuse as they flee, on the way, and in many refugee camps. After being uprooted from their communities and sometimes losing the male head of household to conflict, women need to find new livelihoods to sustain their families in addition to dealing with trauma. The needs are immense and we are trying to fill some of that gap. Through partnerships with local organisations, WfWI provides women with life and

vocational skills trainings, psychosocial therapy, and classes on rights and health. Our work is focused on not only providing women with healing but also with opportunities to thrive, to earn an income, to rebuild lives, and to ensure better futures.

Recently, with support from the UN Trust Fund to End Violence against Women we have been able to increase the number of women we serve. Over the next three years, we will provide psychosocial support services, and life and business skills training to 3000 Syrian and Yezidi women to help them overcome trauma and empower themselves. Through local partners we are working to reach the most vulnerable women in need of support, including those suffering severe emotional trauma, at high risk of violence, and living in extreme poverty.

## WOMEN SUPPORTING WOMEN

I always believed I must use the gifts and privileges I was given to help others – especially those experiencing extreme injustice. It was over the years of working on a wide range of issues such as racism, poverty, economic and social inequality that I saw how deeply gender inequality cuts across all of those. Whether you are in a peaceful country or a war-torn one, or a rich country or an impoverished one, gendered discrimination and inequality is pervasive across all communities to different degrees. It is unacceptable that one out of three women on earth have faced physical or sexual violence; that every year 15 million girls are married before their eighteenth birthday, and that many still call this a 'cultural issue' or a 'domestic decision'. This is a human rights issue and it impacts every one of us.

Secretary Hillary Clinton was the featured speaker at our luncheon in 2017. She spoke to a room of more than 500 guests and urged them to support the work that we do. She lent us her voice and said, 'During the course of my years of working on behalf of these issues, this organisation (WfWI) is one that has really produced results.' She also said that 'Women's rights are the unfinished business of the 21st century.' We agree. There is a lot of work to be done and there are many ways to get it done. I deeply believe that the work that WfWI does is unique and extremely efficient in finishing this business. Our numbers show it too. When a woman joins our program her daily income is $0.34. When she graduates it triples to $1.07. While before joining our program 30 per cent of women use family planning, after the program 87 per cent report using it. Before our program, 10 per cent of the women we work with say they talk to other women about their rights. After our program 89 per cent say they do so. And one of the most fantastic and most empowering parts of our work is that anyone can contribute.

## BEING A GAME CHANGER

Being a Game Changer is the ability to bring people together to act around a vision – that takes listening deeply, charting the collective path, then keeping that arm on the tiller/rudder quite firmly: ready to both hold and change course.

*Laurie's*
# ADVICE

- Believe in yourself (while constantly striving to improve).

- Believe in your vision.

- Challenge your own thinking and inform your decisions with data and with people who disagree with you.

- Embrace error or 'fail forward fast': don't worry about mistakes. Learn from them (and don't make the same one again).

- Have fun! The journey to change is a long one. You have to sustain yourself!

# MOTTO

*Everything can be beautiful if you take the time.*

# AERIN LAUDER

## FOUNDER AND CREATIVE DIRECTOR OF AERIN

*The granddaughter of Estée Lauder, Aerin Lauder has always been surrounded by cosmetics, makeup and fragrance. Her own passion for the industry grew after spending her summers working for the family business, where she still acts as Style and Image Director, leading her to create her own beauty and fragrance collection, AERIN, in 2012.*

"Beauty and fragrance are my heritage and my passion. For as long as I can remember, I've been surrounded by it and completely enthralled by it; it's part of me. When I was in sixth grade, I went to school with all my new lip glosses. Everyone wanted to try them on and I knew then that this was something people really wanted. As for fragrance, I remember getting into the car with my grandmother Estée Lauder, and being aware of her scent. She was always testing different fragrances but she especially loved the fragrance Beautiful. We both shared a passion for flowers, especially roses.

## ESTÉE LAUDER

Estée was an amazing grandmother and friend. She was also an incredible role model and taught me the importance of passion, style, hard work, family and, of course, all things beautiful. She taught me so much and has definitely inspired the person I am today – as both a mother and businesswoman. She taught me the importance of quality and attention to detail and, above all, the value of customer relationships. We also both share a love of roses, beauty and fragrance – things my grandmother shared with me from a very young age.

Her biggest strength was her passion. She was unique because although so many women are driven and passionate, they are not always feminine. She taught me the importance of being feminine and strong. She would always have perfect lipstick and she was brilliant at marketing. She really connected with her consumers, which is so important, and what really set her and the brand apart. She would always say, 'A woman knows what a woman wants.'

## KEEPING IT IN THE FAMILY

I think it's important to surround yourself with people who care about you and who you care about, and working with family is just that. My family supports me but also pushes me to always think ahead and do better. Family can also be very honest, which can be hard, but it is important to know what people really think when creating products.

I spent my summers during college working for the family business, then began my career with The Estée Lauder Companies in 1992 as a member of the Prescriptives marketing team working across programs for the colour, fragrance and skincare businesses. Today I'm the Style and Image Director for the Estée Lauder brand as well as the founder and Creative Director of AERIN. Some of the most important initiatives during my time as Creative Director of Estée Lauder included launching the Sensuous campaign; the first of its kind to include multiple models with Gwyneth Paltrow, Hilary Rhoda, Carolyn Murphy and Elizabeth Hurley. This was a concept that Estée Lauder had never done before and one of the most successful to date. In 2010, we introduced Liu Wen as the first Asian spokesmodel for the brand, making beauty history, and we collaborated with Tom Ford to relaunch one of Estée's most brilliant fragrances, Youth Dew.

The biggest lesson I learned was the importance of finding the balance between work and life. Estée was the first person to teach me how important it is to be passionate and proud of what you do, and always talked about balance. She was so ahead of her time in that she had a career and a family, but always managed to take time out for herself. So that's what I try to do every day.

## CREATING AERIN

I am fortunate to have learned so much from a lifetime in beauty. The time came for me to take those lessons and reinterpret them and pursue my own vision, from my own perspective. AERIN has been an amazing journey. I started the brand in 2012, and it has been the perfect way for me to explore different ways to expand the modern woman's lifestyle and provide the product she needs – from beauty and fashion to lifestyle and home.

I was always asked what's in my makeup bag and felt there was a void in the marketplace for a feminine, effortless beauty brand. This was really what inspired me to create the AERIN Beauty brand. I wanted to explore different ways to expand the modern woman's lifestyle and provide the product she needs – from beauty and fashion to lifestyle and home. I feel very strongly about every product the AERIN brand makes and love to be involved from start to finish. It's my name on the package so I want to make sure it's perfect. My grandmother felt the same way so that's definitely a drive I got from her.

AERIN Beauty is a luxury lifestyle beauty and fragrance brand inspired by effortless style. It is designed for and inspired by women with classic, effortless style, but always with a modern point of view. AERIN Beauty allows women to embrace being feminine and pretty through a curated wardrobe of fragrances and rose essentials that are very personal to the woman who is wearing them.

The AERIN Fragrance Collection is really an expression of my life, my memories and my travels. Whether it's a floral note with a fabulous musk or the idea of something that evokes fresh air and sun with a tropical floral, the combinations are unique and distinctive. My hope is that women can select a scent that evokes their own special memories or experiences.

With the AERIN Rose Cologne Collection, I wanted to share three different rose notes I have enjoyed throughout my life in a collection of scents which offer a lighter, luxurious fragrance for every day, every mood and for any reason. Each fragrance embodies my love of roses in a different way. Bamboo Rose is inspired by the more formal gardens you see in Japan. Garden Rose is my way of capturing the lively and lush garden roses you see in the English countryside. Linen Rose brings me to summers past – back to the Eastern shores of Long Island. Each is tied to a very specific memory and I experience each memory every time I smell each cologne.

The packaging is inspired by natural elements such as stones and flowers. Each fragrance bottle has a different gem in a pretty and soft pastel shade, and includes golden details carefully selected to reflect the spirit of the fragrance. Each carton features an exclusive print design.

## THE CHALLENGES AND SUCCESSES

Balancing everything is one of my biggest challenges – just like other working mothers. It's so important to always try and take time for yourself. If you are happy, everyone around you will be happy. Success is feeling proud and passionate about what you do every day. The values of hard work and determination were instilled in me from a very young age. I was always taught that these two elements are integral to have not only a successful business but a successful life. I am really proud when someone tells me they love my products. Everything we create is a result of a long process so it needs to be extraordinary. And I'm constantly working on new projects and new collaborations that will expand the AERIN brand. I look forward to evolving the future collections with inspiration from my travels. ""

*Aerin's*
# ADVICE

- Stay curious.

- Follow your dreams.

- Whatever you do, do it well.

- Work hard and love what you do.

- Even when you're busy, spend the time to make yourself the most beautiful you can be. You don't need a complicated, time-consuming routine to look beautiful.

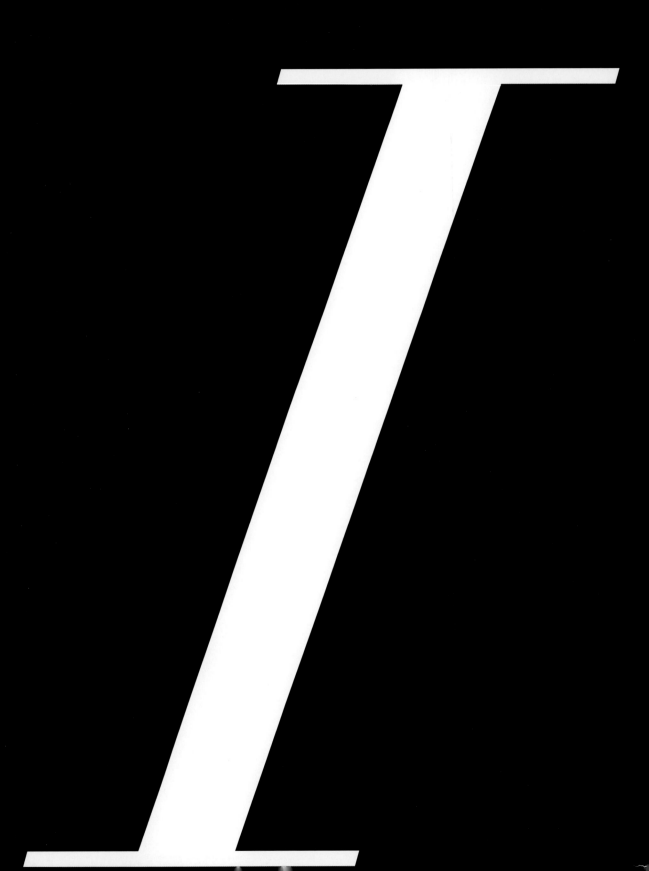

*IF YOU DO WORK YOU LOVE, AND THE WORK FULFILLS YOU, THE REST WILL COME*

**OPRAH WINFREY**

# MOTTO

*I choose happiness.*

# MEGHAN MARKLE

ACTRESS, UNITED NATIONS WOMEN'S ADVOCATE,
FOUNDER AND FORMER EDITOR OF THE TIG

*Meghan Markle is a force to be reckoned with. She is best known for her role as Rachel Zane on the hit US television series* Suits. *She is a World Vision Ambassador and United Nations Women Advocate and is also the founder of the website The Tig, which she describes as 'a hub for the discerning palate' catering to those with a hunger for good food, travel, fashion and beauty.*

I was working for the US Embassy and was going down a path of foreign service. In university, I double majored in Theatre and International Relations, so I knew I loved the energy of both, but wasn't sure where I would settle, career-wise. I was home (in Los Angeles) over the holidays one year, and a manager asked a friend for a student film I had done. She sent it to him and he called me a few days later, saying he wanted to represent me. It was a turning point because I was able to take a step back and re-evaluate what I really wanted to be doing. Plus, truth be told, I was a little homesick at the time, so staying in LA for a bit to roll the dice with an acting career seemed liked a good idea. Thank God it worked!

### *SUITS*

There is just no way of knowing that a show will be a success until it actually becomes one. I had shot five different pilots for various networks that always had amazing buzz. I was convinced they would all get picked up – and none of them did. So when *Suits* came about, I was really drawn to the character, and I loved how intelligent and driven she was – but I also thought I gave a terrible audition. Thankfully, the producers thought otherwise and I booked the role, but it wasn't for several months after filming the first episode that we found out the show was picked up. It was my first pilot that was ever ordered to series, so the phone call from my agent saying it was being greenlit remains one of the best days of my life. Once I got over the shock, that is! I was absolutely paralysed with disbelief.

### RACHEL V MEGHAN

We are both strong willed and driven, as well as being layered and sensitive. I love that as the seasons have progressed, we have gotten past that tough exterior to see how much depth Rachel has, and I appreciate that, as much as she is the moral compass of the show, she is still flawed. I love that it humanises her – she's not perfect. The difference between the two of us is that she certainly cries a lot more than I do, but for good reason. Her life is a tad more dramatic than mine, so I certainly can't judge. What we have in common? Our ambition and our taste in shoes.

### FOUNDING THE TIG

When you spend so much time as an actor saying other people's words for a living, it was really important to me to find a space where I could say my own words. I love that The Tig (www.thetig.com) has become this outlet for me personally, but that it has also become a community of so much support. In my industry it's such a game of smoke and mirrors, of retouching and distortion, that I feel it gives a false message of what young women feel they need to live up to.

Beyond that, I just find it's very important to counteract how much snakiness we find in media and create a space where women support and encourage each other. There's that great quote that I use as a catalyst for my thinking when crafting much of the content on The Tig: 'Girls with dreams become women with vision.' I want The Tig to be part of that narrative – to be part of that vision.

## UNITED NATIONS WOMEN AND WORLD VISION

UN Women reached out to me through The Tig after I wrote a piece on women's empowerment. It was a pleasure to begin working closely with them to advocate for women and girls, and I continue to do that now as Global Ambassador for World Vision, where I recently travelled to Rwanda. Using my hiatus between filming to focus on passion-driven projects and humanitarian work is incredibly valuable to me, and to be honest I'm just really humbled that these organisations entrust me to represent them.

## FITTING EVERYTHING IN

It's a balance, that's for sure! I am self-sufficient and a go-getter, so oftentimes I have to remind myself to take a moment to just breathe. My brain is always going, but at the end of the day because it is all stuff that I am passionate about, it's easier not to feel exhausted as I squeeze it all in. I just hired an assistant for the first time, so hopefully that will help a bit. It feels mighty grown-up, I must say!

## BEING A GAME CHANGER

I started working at a soup kitchen in skid row of Los Angeles when I was thirteen years old, and the first day I felt really scared. I was young, and it was rough and raw down there and, though I was with a great volunteer group, I just felt overwhelmed. I remember one of my mentors (Mrs Maria Pollia) told me that 'life is about putting others' needs above your own fears'. That has always stayed with me. Yes, make sure you are safe and never ever put yourself in a compromising situation, but once that is checked off the list, I think it's really important for us to remember that someone needs us, and that your act of giving/helping/doing can truly become an act of grace once you get out of your head.

# *Meghan's* ADVICE

- Don't give it five minutes if you're not going to give it five years.

- Be kind to yourself.

- Rome wasn't built in a day.

# MOTTO

*Micah 6:8 is a bible verse that guides me. Simply put, 'Act justly, love mercy and walk humbly with the Lord your God.'*

# TAYA KYLE

AUTHOR, FOUNDER OF CHRIS KYLE FROG FOUNDATION

*Taya Kyle is the widow of US Navy Seal, Chris Kyle. She is the co-author of* American Wife: A Memoir of Love, Service, Faith, and Renewal *and was portrayed by Sienna Miller in the Oscar-winning film,* American Sniper. *She is the founder of the Chris Kyle Frog Foundation to help veterans and their families.*

"Originally, my motivation, almost desperation, was to combat my loss by fighting to keep some part of Chris alive. His legacy and his spirit are powerful. I also needed to find my way through the pain, to make a joyful life for my kids. They lost so much when they lost their dad, I didn't want them to lose more of their childhood because of my grief. I am surrounded by people who fight to keep me afloat. I soldier on for them.

My faith is a huge part of my life. I feel God asks us to be the light in other people's darkness. I strive to pay forward the blessings of those who didn't give up on us, by not giving up on other veterans and first responder marriages through my work for the Chris Kyle Frog Foundation.

**GETTING THROUGH THE DARK DAYS**

My friends who were widowed before me showed me that it was possible to walk, or even crawl, after life deals you a crippling blow. No matter how they moved forward or how much they didn't want life to go on, they showed me the strength needed to survive. They showed me the world keeps turning, life goes on, and that healing takes time and courage.

**CHRIS KYLE'S LEGACY**

I was consumed by finishing Chris's work. He was in a difficult place with his company. He had a book called *American Gun* that needed to be finished. He was working on developing a new logo and giving back to veterans and first responders. We were also defending a difficult lawsuit and negotiating different business deals.

My challenge was to be a good mum, to help my kids with their devastation and grief, to absorb the shock and grief for myself, to be a good friend to one of my best friends whose husband was murdered with Chris, and to not let Chris's work fall apart, all while trying to figure out our future. I feel my biggest achievement is my kids' happiness and foundation in faith and love.

**THE MESSAGE**

Know that the gifts you give people have a ripple effect. Some of the people who have helped me the most are people who may never know the impact they have had. For example, my parents and their friends who stayed married over time, just the act of them making their marriages work inspired me to stick through hard times and in turn, inspired the foundation which has helped first responder and military marriages stay together.

For every one of those marriages saved, they help others to do the same. So, sometimes when we can feel it is a man's world or wonder if what we do makes an impact, I hope women will remember the kindness to a person who needs it, being a strong woman, being a joyful mother, aunt or friend. Those things change lives in ways you may never know. Every woman is making her mark; whether she knows it or gets the feedback or not, she is making her mark.

# MOTTO

*There is more in you*
*than you thought.*

# INDIA HICKS

## FOUNDER AND CREATIVE DIRECTOR OF INDIA HICKS, INC

*India Hicks is a former model, the bestselling author of three books and the daughter of David Hicks, one of the world's most celebrated interior designers. She founded her eponymous lifestyle brand India Hicks, Inc in 2015, which encompasses of a range of accessories and fragrances. She is passionate about inspiring women to follow their dreams.*

The major driving force for me is the belief in what I'm doing. I had two unique parents who led individual lives, and both influenced me to think independently. Although I don't think they anticipated I would be the founder of a direct sales company. Or move to an island. Or have five children. Or not learn to speak French with a proper accent!

I started modelling quite late – when I was 19 years old. Most models start much younger now. I once drove down to the countryside with a guest of my father's who happened to be a journalist working for *W Magazine*. He had come to interview my father about his famous garden, and ended up inviting me to be a part of a story called 'New Beauties'. Ralph Lauren spotted me in this feature and flew me first class to California for my first Ralph Lauren job. There were flowers in my room and a warm welcome. From that modelling job, I went to a Winnebago in Florida in 40-degree heat, doing forty shots a day for some dreadful German catalogue, and I realised the real world of modelling was not all like the Ralph Lauren world of modelling.

**Entering The World of Interior Design**

Living under the imposing eye of (my father) David Hicks, I was always a little bit tentative about the world of interior design and finding my own voice. It was only when I moved to a small island in the middle of an ocean and bought our home, Hibiscus Hill, that I was brave enough to decorate it in my own way, and not mimic my father. When a hurricane destroyed a small hotel on the island a few months later, I offered to redecorate and relaunch it, which I did with my other half, David. This project caught quite a lot of media attention and gave me the confidence to really start designing on many different levels and in all sorts of categories.

**India Hicks Inc**

Having had a wonderful licensing career in partnership with other companies, I decided it was time to do something that I could truly own for myself. I designed the collections to be beautifully crafted and also to tell the stories of my life, and the rather mad moments in it. My two partners (because you always need partners in crime) and I knew that those stories might get lost on the cold, hard shelves of retailers. Instead we chose to build the business by partnering with like-minded women who adore the design world and who were looking for a new chapter to their own story. I never imagined myself in the world of direct sales, but now I can't imagine myself anywhere else.

**The Inspirations**

My collections are inspired by my British heritage, my island life and some madcap daydreams. I drew from different stories, moments, absurd adventures and unusual characters I have met, most of whom I am related too! These stories bring the products to life.

I don't have one particular mentor, but I've been inspired by many outstanding people along the way. The partners I mentioned, who have been embedded in the world of business for a long time, shaped the way our company was created and guide me every day. And of course, I look to women who have set an example, by believing in themselves and being passionate about what they do, whether it's writing poetry or managing a hedge fund.

The biggest challenge in my business so far is being taken seriously. Coming from a background where it wasn't necessarily expected for me to work, and being a woman in the workplace were the two main things I had to negotiate. The key to success and longevity is continuously moving forward and never giving up. It certainly isn't easy.

My advice to aspiring entrepreneurs is to get advice. Listen to others. Learn from your mistakes. But always go with your gut.

# *India's top* 5 TIPS

- Act appropriately (which will make some people who know me well laugh, because I swear like a sailor and have the humour of a twelve-year-old).

- Dress appropriately.

- Be the person you hope your daughter looks up to.

- Don't be scared by social media. But don't be controlled by it either.

- And never take a miniature dog into a business meeting.

# MOTTO

*Be authentic.*

# MONIQUE LHUILLIER

FASHION DESIGNER

*Since 1996, Monique Lhuillier has revolutionised the wedding gown industry ith her luxurious, feminine label worn by celebrities and fans across the globe. The label is now internationally recognised as one of the world's foremost couture bridal and ready-to-wear brands.*

I've always been passionate about design and fashion. I grew up in the Philippines with a very glamorous mother. She loved to entertain and I would watch her get dressed, and help her choose outfits and accessories. My mother had also started a children's clothing business – tailor-made special occasion clothes. I learned to choose fabrics, design and fit. Everything about the way I grew up seemed to organically lead me to fashion; the fashion seed was planted early on.

By high school I had already decided I wanted to open my own fashion house and have my own brand with stores around the world. That's what it said in my high school yearbook in 1987! When I graduated I had already determined to study fashion design at FIDM (Fashion Design and Fashion Merchandising in the United States).

When I graduated from FIDM, I was engaged and the search for a wedding dress proved challenging. In bridal at the time there were two extreme trends: overly fussy and detailed, or very stark, modern and minimal. I wanted something that was romantic and traditional with a twist, and I saw a niche in the market. Back then I didn't have a goal, I just wanted to get my business started. I knew that if I was looking for a particular style of wedding dress and I couldn't find it on the market, that other women likely felt the same.

While I was planning my wedding, I was working for a small French company designing ready-to-wear. A year after I was married, I found the courage to leave my job and to try my hand at starting my own label. I had felt at my own wedding that I had really wanted the experience of being pampered. I wanted to have that experience of being a bride and being looked after, and to be honest I didn't really get it. When I opened my first boutique, creating that kind of environment and experience was very important to me.

Once multiple orders started coming in, I realised we had begun. For about three years no one knew how to pronounce my name – then one day they could! I felt we'd finally gained a great following and we were heading in the right direction.

## BUILDING THE BRAND

My husband and I were very young when we got married and one of the best decisions we made was to wait to start our family so we could focus on building our business. We were young and didn't have much experience. In a sense we were lucky that one of us had a design background and the other knew how to run a business. We learned from our mistakes, which could sometimes be expensive, a challenge for any new business. We worked seven days a week, hosting trunk shows on the weekends.

Our goal at the time was first to make a beautiful product, and then build a luxury brand. As soon as we could, we sought to put together a strong team so we could expand with that support. I didn't think at the time that I would grow into a lifestyle brand including Home and Beauty, I didn't think that far ahead.

At the height of Britney Spears's career, making her bridal gown created an enormous amount of exposure for my brand. Britney wanted to collaborate on the design and feel of her gown, so I created something I thought expressed her personality as a bride and made her feel that day was special.

Also, identifying a niche in the market, and focusing on a beautiful product were integral to my early success and longevity. Great relationships within the industry have certainly been inherent in our ability to grow. We were determined and committed to the growth of the business.

## THE GROWTH

We started with the intention to develop a successful bridal business, and to open our own retail locations. My dresses were feminine and traditional, with a modern twist. They were cut very close to the body, which gave them a more youthful energy. Intricate detail with an ethereal lightness was important to me in design and developed as a signature of my bridal collections. I'm inspired by living, travel, fabric, art, a beautiful piece of embroidery. I like to create a romance and theatre with my designs, so the starting point is often a mood or a feeling.

I've been fortunate to design for some incredible women for special moments in their life. I've also enjoyed dressing high-profile women, who throughout my career have helped take my brand to a larger audience. When I see women in my clothes, it validates what I do.

When we reached a great rhythm in bridal, we look at our customer and her life beyond the wedding and looked at how we could grow with her. The next step was launching evening and ready-to-wear and diffusion lines. My fashion categories now also include fur, accessories, footwear and eyewear.

After twenty years in business I am proud to have a brand that encompasses fashion and lifestyle, bridal mainline and two diffusions, engagement rings with Blue Nile. Ready-to-wear presents four collections a year and diffusion. Lifestyle covers fine paper to home fragrance, fine crystal, collaborations in home decor specifically for children, and most recently my first beauty collaboration. My designs have an incredible representation in retail across the US and internationally – Neiman Marcus has been an amazing partner from the beginning. I'm also proud to have two flagship stores in New York and LA, and would like to open more Monique Lhuillier doors. Bergdorf Goodman, Harrods and Saks Fifth Avenue have also been strong supporters from the very beginning.

# Monique's 5 TIPS

- Stay focused on your product and protective of its integrity.

- Determination is key.

- Value relationships – you can't build a successful business without wonderful partnerships along the way.

- Be committed and consistent.

- Go with your gut.

## THE BABY RANGE

Images had been published of my home, including my children's rooms, so people had seen my space and home design. Pottery Barn Kids reached out for a collaboration because they knew my brand and thought I might be interested in extending my design philosophy into the realms of decor. It was exciting for me to look at how we grow with this family and how well my aesthetic could translate to children's furniture. With a few children I had the authority to know what that looked like, and my own experience inspired the collection. As a mother I knew what I needed from the practical pieces in my kids' rooms. It opened my mind to another design category that was so fun to explore.

## THE BALANCING ACT

My husband and I were very lucky we waited to start a family. We had been married for eleven years, and had already laid the foundation and the groundwork for our company, so creating that balance was easier. I felt strongly about not changing our life entirely for children, but inviting them into the world we had created. I'm so proud to be able to show my children that it is possible to have a rewarding career and a rich family life – it is something we work very hard at every day.

My down time is about being with my family. I like to travel with my family, and expose my children to different places and cultures. It's a joy to see new experiences through their eyes. Family is my greatest achievement. Being a good wife and mother, a good friend is important to me. In my career, being able to empower women to feel confident and beautiful in my clothes has been a huge accomplishment. My advice is to focus on what you're passionate about, to be determined and consistent. Be authentic to who you are, because if you aren't, people can see right through that.

*SUCCESS BEGINS
AT THAT MAGICAL
MOMENT WHEN YOU
DECLARE TO
YOURSELF, YOUR
FRIENDS AND THE
UNIVERSE THAT
YOU BELIEVE YOU
CAN DO SOMETHING
DIFFERENT*

**NATALIE MASSENET**

# MOTTO

*To have the passion of a storyteller,
the resilience of a entrepreneur and
the creativity of an artist. That is how
I want to live my life and the person
I want to be.*

# JO MALONE

FOUNDER OF JO LOVES

*Jo Malone is a pioneer in the fragrance industry, creating her eponymous line of fragrances and luring a cult-like following of customers in the mid 90s, before selling to Estée Lauder. In 2011 she launched Jo Loves, a fragrance brand designed to capture the inspirations in Jo's life.*

I think everybody has something in life that they are really good at. There are lots of things I can't do, but I have an amazing sense of smell. Everything I see translates into smell; I see colour in smell, I hear music in smell… basically for me, everything translates into fragrance notes. It's like a language for my nose.

Ever since I was a ten-year-old girl, I would experiment with different smells, mixing oils and flowers from my garden on my stove to learn how they worked together.

I started out my career as a beauty therapist at age twenty-two, doing facials from my tiny apartment in London, where I was running around in a little white coat. We didn't have two pennies to rub together, so all I had was a massage bed. I had no actual bed in my apartment, just a blue foam mattress that I would put away during the day, and bring out at night. We had no furniture either, but I was able to transform this tiny little place into a spa that clients seemed to love.

## HUMBLE BEGINNINGS

I started off with a dozen clients. They would climb three flights of stairs to my little salon where they would have their face done. I wanted to make my own face cream, so I started mixing oils that I had made in Paris to use on the women. In the early days, I would experiment with essential oils including jojoba, avocado, rosemary…

The business took off when I created a nutmeg and ginger body lotion that I would give to clients as a gift, and the women loved it! I was massaging people's arms with it after their facials and everyone wanted to buy the body lotion. Twelve clients grew to twenty clients within a week through word of mouth. I didn't have money for a bed, let alone advertising and marketing, but I started getting the beauty editors of major magazines through and that is primarily how word spread.

Kathy Phillips, who was the fashion director of *Tatler* magazine, wanted to write an article about me – and that was the start of something unbelievable. The article was titled, 'Scenter of the Universe' and created such a buzz and demand that when we opened up our first store in October 1994, there was a line around the block.

From there, newspapers across the country wanted to write about us; the *Financial Times*, British *Vogue* … and the demand grew and grew for the products that I had invented in my tiny little kitchen. And it wasn't just in the UK – the whole world wanted them!

The original packaging was very simple – just little plastic bottles. I would go down to a warehouse and pick up six crates of boxes filled with bottles, create labels on the typewriter and go down to the local printer to get them printed. I would give each product out in little white Chinese takeaway boxes. The orders began to pour in and that was the moment I knew that the Jo Malone brand was about to take off. From there, we just grew and grew.

## SELLING JO MALONE LONDON

Often businesses reach a point where they grow so rapidly, you can feel it backfiring. Within five years of opening our first store, we sold the business to Estée Lauder. When people ask me why I sold the business, I tell them that growth can start to backfire. So I was looking for a company with deep pockets, distribution and heart – I needed someone that really loved me and loved the industry. I could find the first two – money and distribution – but it's that last ingredient – the heart – that completes the triangle for growth.

I met Leonard Lauder in 1999, and when I signed a deal to hand Jo Malone London over, I honestly thought I was going to stay with the company forever. It was just a happy time. But eighteen months into it I was diagnosed with breast cancer. And that changed everything for

me. I was given a very poor diagnosis and told that I didn't have that long. I had to have surgery, so I decided to go to America and lived for a year in New York fighting the cancer. I came out a very different person. I felt I didn't belong in the company anymore. And so I exited in 2006.

When I left Estée Lauder in 2006, I knew I had made a huge mistake. I remember that last moment, putting the last bottle on the shelf and turning the key in the door. It was announced in the press and it was too late to say that I had changed my mind. This is a huge lesson to myself and others – sometimes we make big mistakes, but it doesn't mean to say you can't go on and still fulfill your dreams. I had agreed to a five year lock out – but as a creator and artist, the thought of not creating anything in five years was probably one of the worst things I had done for myself. So much so that for a couple of years I wouldn't even walk through a cosmetics store – it was just too emotional!

Then one day I was walking through Harrods, and I opened a jar of a beauty product and smelt it, and I felt tears welling up in my eyes. I knew I would have to go back to the industry. I tried to write myself a CV, but mine was just so awful. I felt so humiliated. I didn't know who to call for someone to give me a job. I would have done anything in the cosmetics industry but I just had no confidence. I lost who Jo Malone was: the spirit of Jo. And I was so unhappy.

## CREATING 'JO LOVES'

When the five year lockout came to an end, I thought I was going to make television. So I created a reality television show called *High Street Dreams*, about entrepreneurs. For one of the episodes I was standing with a family filling bottles of chili sauce at their home and I had a white coat on and a hair net – and I think it was filling the bottles and seeing this family's passion, and the reminder of the original white coat I used to wear, that I just knew then and there that I just had to try one more time in the industry I was so passionate about.

At that moment it wasn't about building a global brand – just about doing something that I was passionate about and that I loved. A few days later, as I sat around a kitchen table, I wondered what it would mean if I did it all again. So I put together a concept, went to the head counsel of Estée Lauder and showed them so they didn't get any surprises, and then sat down and worked out what I was going to do next.

In 2011, I launched Jo Loves. It was hard work! At first I got the packaging wrong, I got the fragrances wrong. It is really important for people to understand that despite entrepreneurs looking like they get it right the first time, they often get it wrong. But they push till they get it right. And that's exactly what I did. Now I am so proud that I did; I look at this brand and I am so proud of it.

The Jo Loves Pomelo fragrance was our first fragrance, and it symbolised to me that I could do this again. It is the hope of another chapter in my life and it is a symbol to me that my dream of changing the world with fragrance is very much alive.

## THE LAUNCH

We started Jo Loves in a studio by invitation only – and I was so surprised by the number of people wondering around trying to find the studio! We then did a pop up shop in Selfridges. We had created a hunger around the brand; there was an ever-growing tribe that spread the message to help make the brand strong and powerful, so people are driven into department stores saying they want it. That's now happening in the Middle East, New York, China, Mumbai, India and all over America. Net-a-Porter has helped spread the word too. They have those qualities I was talking about before: distribution, deep pockets and heart. They were able to take our brand and put it into the hands of people who share the same market and clientele as Jo Loves. Emirates airline has also been a huge supporter, promoting the product in its duty free line. Next we will be changing the way the world wears fragrance.

## WHAT MAKES JO A GAME CHANGER

I'm not frightened of being the only one standing that believes in my dream. I will stand alone if I have to.

# Jo's top
# *TIPS*

- Success is about 10 per cent inspiration, 90 per cent perspiration.

- Fix your mind on your goal. Every single day the world changes, people change. Head towards your dream.

- When you fall down and fail, pick yourself back up and start walking towards your goal. You have to have the motivation.

- Enjoy the journey.

- When you have succeeded – don't forget to think to yourself how lucky you are.

- Don't think you're owed it, but that you've earned it and it's your right.

# MOTTO

*Reflect rather than react.*

# OLIVIA PALERMO

ENTREPRENEUR

*Olivia Palermo is an international fashion and beauty icon, who found fame after being cast in the reality television series* The City, *which followed the professional lives of young women based in New York City. She has since graced the covers of dozens of magazines across the globe and has cemented herself as a true style icon of her generation.*

Even at a young age, I was passionate about fashion and naturally sought to grow within an industry that I loved. I began by studying at the American University in Paris where I was fortunate enough to receive my first professional experience as an intern at *Quest* magazine. It was there that I gained insight into how a magazine should run along with learning first hand about all the different facets within the industry.

At *Quest*, I had the opportunity to work with the magazine's Market Editor, which involved discovering new designers, meeting with interior decorators, and finding interesting venues for various projects. It was a wonderful way for me to get exposure within the fashion and editorial worlds, giving me a strong foundation for future positions, like at *Elle* magazine, and helping me to gain insight into what possible directions I wanted to take my career towards.

### THE CITY

Intitially, Viacom contacted my former agent to inquire whether I would be interested in participating in the reality television show *The City*. The show was not what I expected

because of the scripting; however, the decision to participate in the show was not difficult and I might not be where I am today if I had turned down the opportunity. The show's exposure allowed me to be heard and recognised on a global scale, which was a unique opportunity for me at that time.

I received an intern role at Diane von Furstenberg as part of filming the show. I look up to so many women in and out of the industry but I have always held Diane von Furstenberg in high regard. I feel as though she is a pioneer for a certain type of woman in the market and has done so much for emerging talent, so it was great to get to work with her.

After the show, I focused full-time with Wilhelmina International, a talent and model management agency, to build my brand.

**BUILDING THE OLIVIA PALERMO BRAND**

The motivation behind my website, oliviapalermo.com, was to document travel locations that I enjoyed as well as to build a platform using my own voice for style. Subsequently, it has evolved into a lifestyle and editorial website reflecting my aesthetic while supporting emerging, young designers. Each year, on average, the website attracts an audience of passionate supporters from over 220 countries.

I currently work with many different brands including campaigns for AERIN and

## *Olivia's top* *TIPS*

- Try different roles within an industry in order to decide the path you would like to pursue.

- Let your hard work speak for itself.

- Always be pulled together as it sets your mind to be productive.

MAX&Co, and on a larger scale as Global Brand Ambassador for Banana Republic. In addition to my ambassador role, I have co-designed a capsule collection with Banana Republic launching in Fall 2017. We're a great team and it's been a collaborative approach that reflects the synergy between my style and the Banana Republic brand. Overall, I believe my brand represents an ever-evolving, fresh perspective to contemporary classics that is relatable to women of all ages.

## GETTING SOCIAL

My view of social media has evolved and I have learned from experience and continue to do so. Whereas before it would be an outfit post or a piece of jewellery that I liked, it is now such a useful tool to share what I think about fashion, beauty and culture. It's great to be able to communicate with designers and users in a new way. I can express myself and my style – whether it be a picture on Instagram, sharing a story on my website or providing inspiration for an upcoming shoot on Pinterest. I think it is fascinating how direct and powerful these social media platforms have become for myself and my brand.

## THE CHALLENGES

I face challenges everyday head-on, which helps me learn more and allows me to continue evolving. I feel that a big contributor to my success has been surrounding myself with a smart, tight-knit team as they are a reflection of myself and my brand. This has enabled me to build and grow a brand that is organic and true to my vision. As for the future of my brand? You will have to wait and see!

# MOTTO

*I live by the belief that you can learn something from every single person you meet; you are never too wise or too old to learn something new.*

# NATASHA OAKLEY

FOUNDER OF A BIKINI A DAY, MONDAY SWIMWEAR AND MONDAY ACTIVE

*Sporting one of the world's most envied bodies, Natasha Oakley has made a business out of wearing beautiful bikinis in beautiful destinations, creating a worldwide phenomenon with the first-ever bikini blog titled A Bikini A Day, run alongside best friend Devin Brugman, that spawned a swimwear and an activewear label coveted by their fans across the world.*

"I created the A Bikini A Day blog with my best friend Devin Brugman in Los Angeles. We realised we had a serious obsession with swimwear and the life that surrounds it, and wanted to share it with the world. It was really a passion project to begin with!

Before we started the blog, I had my own production company and was actually shooting swimwear campaigns in Hawaii and Los Angeles. I think we can attribute the professional quality of our images from the early days to the fact that both Devin and I had experience with photography.

**BUILDING THE BRAND**

People instantly took to the concept of A Bikini A Day – we found that there was something for everyone to relate to, whether it was the friendship between Devin and me, our travels, our entrepreneurialism or our personal style. In 2012, it was a fairly new concept to be documenting your life professionally on Instagram so there was naturally a huge interest in the consistent content we were creating. Our content was a reflection of our lifestyle and I

think people really just gravitated towards it for obvious reasons; because the beach and warm weather appeal to most people! Also, there wasn't (at that stage) any kind of online platform that was dedicated to showcasing the latest suits from our favourite swimwear brands. It's always beneficial to know how something looks on different body types before you purchase online, and we provided that.

We noticed pretty soon after A Bikini A Day started to gain followers that a lot of the young women who were following us were feeling inspired by the way we were comfortable in our own skin. It was a real eye opener for us, and we loved that we were able to help girls feel more confident within themselves to be in a bikini on the beach – which can be a very daunting thing.

## THE SUPPORT NETWORK

I have an amazing group of people in my life who are very supportive and understanding of my career. I grew up with parents who each own their own businesses and provided me with insight into the world of entrepreneurialism. But actually, the fact that my best friend is also my business partner was the kind of help you can't pass up, and the kind that doesn't come around too often. Devin was my moral support as well as my business partner – we make an amazing team and it wouldn't have been the same without her.

I think the key to our success was that we were providing something that didn't exist yet. We found our niche without actually looking for one, within an industry that was just becoming a legitimate career path: blogging and social media. We worked really hard to pursue what we viewed as an extremely unique opportunity for ourselves at that point in our lives, so I think it was a combination of our effort and innovativeness that was the key to our success. The photos, the clothes, the destinations? Yes, these beautiful things really do exist in our lives but we are extremely appreciative of every opportunity we are given and always have been. Even in the early days when we weren't travelling the world and receiving gifts from amazing designers, we felt like the luckiest girls in the world just for the simple fact that we were able to create our own career paths.

## A TYPICAL DAY

This is the million dollar question! A typical workday for us varies from place to place, but our love for the beach definitely keeps us in check and on top of our game. The beach is our play-ground and our office, so when we're there we make sure to shoot as much as we can.

It's a win-win! An average A Bikini A Day shoot includes around 50–60 bikinis in one day.

## THE LABELS

Creating our own swimwear was a natural progression for us – wearing literally hundreds of suits a year gives you a pretty good idea of what's out there and what's missing. Monday Swimwear really is a product of our environment. We wanted to design suits that had longevity: classic, timeless pieces that were made for all figures. Monday Active was born of the same concept. Activewear should be comfortable, supportive and stylish in order for women to feel confident when they're working out. Monday Swimwear and Active share the same notion aesthetically, which is important for us so that our friends and followers know what to expect across the board from our brands.

Our biggest hurdles are conceptualising these designs without sacrificing style, quality or comfort – but we think we do a pretty great job! Apart from that we have had to learn the ins and outs of an industry that was completely new to us. We do not have partners in our brand so every aspect of the business is managed by us: the design, production, manufacturing, ecommerce sites etc.

## THE CONTROVERSY

I was taken aback when the issue of airbrushing dropped in the media as I was completely misquoted. The question I had been confronted with in the interview was, 'Why do you think social media influencers are editing their images?' My response was, 'I think people are trying to mimic what they see in the media.' It was quite satirical how my words got twisted in that interview and apparently became an 'admission' – but I really wasn't threatened by it. My business is bikinis. I'm in a swimsuit 90 per cent of the year, attend appearances all over the world, conduct photoshoots weekly, etc ... There is nothing my photographs can say about myself or my body that people don't see in reality. I felt so supported during that time, and I knew the only opinions that mattered were of the people who know me, like my friends and followers.

In terms of feeling the pressure to look the part – looking good and feeling good are one in the same, really. I feel better in all aspects of my life when I'm

working out consistently. It's challenging to find time, which is why I opt for HIIT (High Intensity Interval Training) workouts that suit my busy schedule, and it makes all the difference to my energy levels – I'm not sure I could lead such a hectic lifestyle without the energy I gain from training. There is obviously pressure in the media and online to always look your best, but it doesn't effect me negatively. I'm not afraid of criticism, I have a pretty thick skin which is important in this industry. I just make sure I am doing what I know is best for me and it seems to work in my favour. I encourage people to do the same in that respect.

## COLLABORATIONS

I have to be selective with the brands and companies I collaborate with because the nature of my work means it is a direct reflection of my personality and beliefs. I am approached by a huge number of brands every week! But the truth is, my schedule is crazy, I live between three major cities and travel at least 80 per cent of the year. Aside from choosing brands that reflect my own style, and are in line with my own brand both aesthetically and morally, I have to coordinate any collaborations according to my schedule. If there were three more of me I could potentially look at working with all of my most loved brands!

My favourite collaboration so far is the collection I designed for GUESS. The collection itself was inspired by vintage GUESS swimwear worn by the likes of Claudia Schiffer and Anna Nicole Smith, and the campaign was shot in black and white, true to some of the most iconic GUESS photo shoots.

## THE CHALLENGES

Deciding how much is too much when it comes to business is probably my biggest challenge. I'm very passionate about my business and I find it difficult to switch off. I think most people who have a business of their own, or any kind of passion, would feel the same way. My business is like my baby – I want to make sure I'm nurturing it in every way I can and helping it to grow and be successful, which requires me to be on the clock at all hours of the day and night. My situation of running the business as well as being the face of it is extremely unique – I am solely responsible for my own success and there is no one that can take my place in that position.

And fitting everything in! I have to select jobs according to my schedule and locations throughout the year. I have jobs lined up over the next couple of years, so it can definitely feel overwhelming at times. Unfortunately I do have to turn down jobs quite often, but I have to be conscious to not 'spread myself too thin' as the saying goes. I commit myself fully to the jobs and collaborations I take on and want to make sure I can always perform to the best of my ability.

# Tash's
# *ADVICE*

- Remain true to yourself. I know it's a cliché, and maybe even overstated, but it's completely true. People are attracted to authenticity and can very easily sense when someone is not necessarily passionate about what they are sharing with the world.

*WE HAVE TO RESHAPE OUR OWN PERCEPTION OF HOW WE VIEW OURSELVES. WE HAVE TO STEP UP AS WOMEN AND TAKE THE LEAD*

**BEYONCÉ**

# MOTTO

*A mentor of mine, whom I respect enormously and runs a multi-million dollar global fashion empire, has always said to me, 'Just say yes.' When opportunities arise, your default response should be yes. Sometimes things do not work out but always being open to ideas and opportunities can only lead to progress.*

# JULIE STEVANJA

## FOUNDER AND CEO OF STYLERUNNER

*The creator of an ecommerce store for fitness fanatics, Julie Stevanja has been credited for inspiring the 'sports luxe' craze with her online activewear retailer Stylerunner. The site grew by almost 2000 per cent in the first three years, generating a cult-like following. Winner of Young Retailor of the Year and named in the Deloitte Tech Top 50, Stylerunner is firmly cemented as the go-to site for activewear fantatics, delivering to customers in more than 100 countries around the globe.*

Before I started Stylerunner, I was living in London working for a tech start-up called MUBI. It's a streaming video on-demand platform for cult, foreign and arthouse film. Think Netflix for hipsters! My time at MUBI gave me the start-up bug. We had to be agile, hustle, iterate quickly. Before that, my first professional role was in Institutional Finance at ANZ, which gave me a great grounding for business, planning, and risk mitigation. Even my time selling advertising at *Vogue Living* was useful. I was not there for long, but I had to learn to sell, pick up the phone and cold call, meet face-to-face with clients and get them over the line. In a start-up you're selling every single day!

## CREATING STYLERUNNER

The idea for Stylerunner was born really out of a personal need more than anything else. I was religiously attending Bikram yoga five times a week and was finding it really hard to buy fashionable activewear, so that's really where the idea for Stylerunner came from.
I kept going back to the idea of an online destination carrying beautiful premium activewear. I reasoned that if I was facing this problem, then there were likely many others in the same position – this was well before activewear as we know it today become a 'thing'!

The online business model also seemed to work well specifically for the activewear category (targeting time poor professionals) and my background in tech start-ups gave me the confidence to launch Stylerunner. The name was the result of some extensive brain mapping and searching for available domain names. After narrowing down a short list, I ran them past some close friends and Stylerunner was the winner – it was also the most expensive at $2800!

## BUILDING THE BRAND

Social media was crucial for Stylerunner in its infancy, but the truth to traction is finding 'product-market-fit' – i.e. building a great solution to a real problem. If you can't seem to get traction, don't focus on growing, focus on validating your idea and do whatever you need to do get get product-market-fit – stop and hold a focus group, call some potential customers, and work out what you need to tweak to help the customer. Having worked at a tech start-up previously, I was fortunate to have some insight into the tech elements, but there were also moments when my head would spin from new information. I was determined, however, to understand every aspect of my business. It took time and many long calls to tech consultants and mentors, but I learned so much, especially in those first few years. When you're not working in a start-up, you should be learning!

A great moment was when we began working with the big players in the industry, Nike and Adidas. When they were as enthusiastic about our business model as we were I knew then that we were on the right track. There was nobody really offering the point of difference and dedication to fashion-meets-activewear that we were championing at that time so it was filling a gap in the market.

Of course, like anyone launching a start-up, there never seem to be enough hours in the day and the 'to-do' list never seems to end. The key is to work on what's important, not what's urgent. I use Eisenhower's Quadrant to help manage this. Beyond that though, sound financial management is crucial and walking the line between investing in your growth and being careful not to overspend is something that takes time to master! I cannot stress the importance of getting the right advice in this department. I think that we got into the market at a great time when the fashion consumer was really starting to explore a more balanced life, and fitness formed a big part of that. In addition to this, social media has enabled us to form a relationship with our customers in a way that brands could not do in the past. Through this, Stylerunner has really become more than just an online shopping space, it has become a resource for health and fitness and a community that our customers can engage with on many levels. That is one of the most exciting parts for me.

# *Julie's top* TIPS

- Have a plan and write it down.

- Look at that plan every day and make decisions based on those goals.

- Surround yourself with the right people but always trust your instincts. If it doesn't feel right, don't do it.

- Network, network, network. Meet as many people you can in your chosen field, you never know where a conversation can lead.

- Just start. Do not procrastinate. Nothing will ever be perfect the first time but once you have started, the rest will follow.

## CEMENTING THE 'SPORT LUXE' TREND

Fashion designers have been doing sport-inspired collections forever, but I think what we were able to do was simply build what was already there into a dedicated destination to ensure the best of this category was always available. I really think that people in general are becoming more aware of and focused on their mental and physical wellbeing so the growth of the category was always going to happen. We have definitely had some incredible 'pinch me' moments. I never thought we'd be listed amongst the country's top tech start-ups in Deloitte Tech 50 or BRW Fast Starters. Winning the Young Retail Entrepreneur of the Year at the World Retail Awards was a highlight though! Developing talent and watching young, whip-smart future leaders grow in confidence has to be one of the best parts of running a business. I'm also grateful that it has opened doors to meet inspiring, successful founders and businesspeople around the world. It's kind of like a money-can't-buy club! I guess being a Game Changer is about having faith in yourself first and foremost.

## BEING A GAME CHANGER

You will encounter a huge number of people, friends, family, colleagues and even experts, who question what you plan to do. It takes courage and resilience but most importantly a very strong sense of self and belief in your abilities, determination and experience to forge your own way into the unknown.

My advice to aspiring entrepreneurs is have passion for what you are doing. The long days are endless and there may be many months of sacrificing time with your partner, family and friends before you even make any money so you need to love it or you will struggle to last the distance! It's not all doom though, when you do reach a goal, even if just a little one, the satisfaction you feel is empowering and drives you forward to reach the next one.

# MOTTO

*Common sense.*

# MELISSA ODABASH

FASHION DESIGNER

*A former swimwear model, Melissa Odabash launched her eponymous swimwear collection in 1999. The collection swiftly came to epitomise the glamour and sophistication of a luxury lifestyle brand and was named by British* Vogue *as 'the Ferrari of the bikini world'. Her label is distributed in over forty-eight countries and sold in over 250 luxury department stores. It is a favourite line of many A-list stars including Kate Moss, Gwyneth Paltrow, Beyoncé and the Duchess of Cambridge.*

I got into the fashion industry through modelling – I was scouted at a young age and moved to Europe to pursue my modelling career. I was living in Italy and realised that everything I was modelling was too rash or too revealing. The prints and styles were not doing any justice for a woman's body, so I decided to create my own line using high quality fabrics and simple colours that would suit any woman with any shape.

I wanted to create something that was classic and timeless. I learned from the swimwear business which fabrics worked and which ones were the better choices for swimwear. I sought out information from buyers to find out what they were looking for when buying swimwear. In addition, I travelled and lived in many countries so I was able to understand the different markets and demands from customers in these locations. I started out by going from door to door with my samples in Italy, which was tough. Getting paid in Italy was even harder!

## BUILDING THE BRAND

A year or so into designing, a friend of mine managed to take some samples of my work over to the United States and managed to get them into *Sports Illustrated* magazine. Seeing my designs on Tyra Banks and Naomi Campbell in the *Sports Illustrated* calendar was an amazing moment for me. Then, two years later, Victoria's Secret stocked one of my designs – a zebra print with a blue border – and this really helped brand awareness grow!

Over the years, my brand has continued to evolve and I feel very lucky to have hit many milestones, but I have to say having won several awards in the last couple of years has been such a great time. I won Swimwear Designer of the Year in London, Designer of the Year in Paris and Retailer of the Year very recently. It's great to be recognised after fifteen years of hard work.

## THE FUTURE

Next, I will be launching a ready-to-wear collection, which I am very excited about! I will also be launching more accessories that will complement my core lines.

# Melissa's
# *ADVICE*

- Never give up focus!

- Choose one product and get it right.

- Once you have mastered the first product, then look to expand.

- Don't do anything just for money, do it for your passion and money will come later. At least you will love doing what you do!

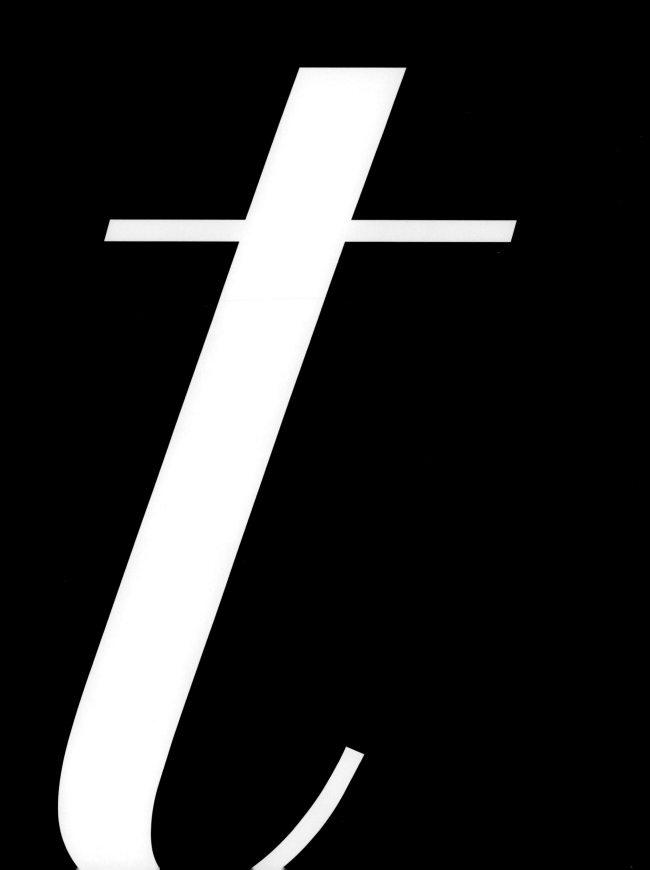

# THE QUESTION ISN'T WHO IS GOING TO LET ME; IT'S WHO IS GOING TO STOP ME

AYN RAND

# MOTTO

*Dream big.*

# SOPHIA WEBSTER

## SHOE DESIGNER

*Sophia Webster is a British shoe designer celebrated for her playful designs and loved by fashion editors and fashionistas alike.*

**B**efore I studied for my Foundation in Art at Camberwell College, I used to dance. My sister and I would travel around the country and compete in national competitions. I still fit in a couple of dance classes a week – it's something I really enjoy.

When I studied at Camberwell College, I did a lot of still life drawing and found that I loved drawing shoes more than anything else. From there, I enrolled in the BA Footwear Design course at Cordwainers College and didn't look back. I went on to do my masters at The Royal College of Art where I discovered the kind of brand I wanted to have. I wanted to position my brand for a market I felt hadn't been reached, so women could buy designer shoes at an accessible price point. My brand is really versatile and caters for women who are fashion forward and excited to wear lace-up flamingos on their feet, as well as women who are perhaps a little more classic and want to wear a simple pump with an interesting detail.

## THE CHALLENGES

It was definitely challenging finding the infrastructure for my business, particularly the factory. I considered manufacturing in China and there were also lots of things I could have had made in Italy, but it meant that the shoes would be too expensive for my market. I wanted to identify the right factory that could create luxury shoes at an affordable price range. I wanted my line to begin at £250 and increase in price for more special styles. Because of this, I ended up finding an incredible team at a factory in Brazil who I still work with to this day.

From the beginning, they were willing to take me and my very small orders on and over the last three years we have been on a really exciting journey together. They are proud to be producing shoes that are stocked in the best stores around the world and I am proud to showcase the exceptional quality of Brazilian manufacturing. I visit the factory as much as I can and love going there – the culture of the country is so inspiring.

## GETTING THE WORD OUT

I was very fortunate that I started the company around the same time that Instagram was starting, so from the beginning, I've been able to communicate with women globally and have that direct interaction with my customers. A huge amount of thought goes into our social media platforms and I feel we definitely get a lot back for that extra effort.

## THE FUTURE

I feel my biggest achievements have been winning the 2016 Vogue Designer Fashion Fund and opening my first store on Mount St, London. I want to keep on expanding the business and the team, as well as rolling out more stores globally in key destinations. I'm looking forward to continuing to grow my online business and social media channels.

# Sophia's
# *ADVICE*

- Trust yourself, stay true to your own vision, but also be willing to take a step back and look at the bigger picture sometimes.

- It's really important to take the emotion out of how you deal with tricky situations; be assertive, direct and focus your energy on moving forward.

MOTTO

*Beat yesterday.*

# JENNIFER FISHER

## JEWELLERY DESIGNER

*From Hollywood stylist to jewelry entrepreneur and mother of two, Jennifer Fisher has proved anything is possible. From a one-person business, she has grown Jennifer Fisher Jewelry into a global multi-million dollar brand.*

My styling career was a lucky break. I studied Business Marketing at USC with a Fine Art minor. I was convinced I wanted to work on the advertising side at a fashion magazine. During a brief internship of watching the other interns in the fashion department roll racks of designer clothing by as I was crunching ad numbers, I knew I was on the wrong side of the magazine. I began assisting a few celebrity stylists that unfortunately were not the easiest to work for. As luck may have it, my best friend was working at the time at Propaganda Films under a commercial director who needed a new wardrobe stylist. Timing is truly everything. I took to chance and accepted the job without any commercial styling experience. After my first commercial with him, I became his regular stylist and we spent the next ten years working together working on major national ad campaigns from American Express to Budweiser. For me it was more about the larger branded commercials than celebrities. I could book multiple ad campaigns with multiple sets of assistants and it was an amazing ride. The biggest challenge at this time was managing all the different jobs and travel.

I was diagnosed with my desmoid tumor while I was living and styling in NYC for an LA based director. I received multiple rounds of chemotherapy at Cedars Sinai in Los Angeles and at St Vincents in New York. I worked throughout the entire process. Being diagnosed with anything is always scary. But finding out I had a very rare tumor with no guaranteed form of treatment was the scariest time of my life. It changes everything. From that moment on, your outlook on every day of your life is different.

My husband Kevin proposed to me in the middle of my chemotherapy treatment one night before a big Halloween party at our West Village apartment. We were married a year later – six months after I finished my treatment. When we wanted to have children, my oncologist didn't think it was a good idea for me to carry the baby because my tumor grows from estrogen – so we went through the process of hiring a surrogate to carry for us in California, where Kevin and I both grew up and our families still live. After multiple rounds of IVF where the surrogate was pregnant twice and miscarried twice, I came back to New York and decided to try IVF on my own, against my doctor's orders. Unsuccessful yet again, they recommended that we adopt or get an egg donor. We needed a break from it all and took the summer off. That's when I became pregnant with my son Shane, naturally. Against the wishes of my oncologist I carried the baby. A perfectly healthy pregnancy and baby boy later, we learned that my tumor had actually shrunk during the pregnancy.

## CREATING THE BRAND

After Shane was born, I began receiving jewellery gifts to represent him in the form of single letters that were very dainty and frankly not my style. His birth was a major deal for Kevin and me, and I wanted something to wear that represented him in a way that felt like me. Being a stylist makes you pretty resourceful, so I went up to 47th street in the jewellery district in New York and began knocking on doors, working out how I could create something myself.

My first piece of jewellery was a dog tag to represent my son Shane. After unsuccessfully searching for that ideal piece of jewellery, I had taken it upon myself to make my own. I was wearing the dog tag every day while on set styling and started to get multiple requests for the same necklace. I then happened to make a necklace for Uma Thurman that she ended up wearing on the cover of *Glamour* magazine. Thus, Jennifer Fisher Jewelry was born.

I started a website selling fine jewellery direct to consumer very early on. This gave the line global reach. I truly believe that the early timing of this coincided with the beginning of the online shopping boom, resulting in a happy accident.

After six years of only selling fine jewellery, I was lucky to have garnered a pretty significant following. In order to offer jewellery to a growing customer base, I decided to expand the line with the launch of the brass collection, focusing on large statement pieces at a more accessible price point. We mainly focus on 14K yellow gold and use a process of lost wax casting for our charms and brass statement pieces. The fine collection focuses on 14K and 18K white, rose and yellow gold.

My design process is a bit different to other jewelers as I am inspired by architecture, furniture, lighting design as well as photography.

## EXPANDING THE BRAND

Barneys New York was our first US brick and mortar. Net-a-Porter followed soon after. We have been approached by other US and international retailers but we like to keep our retail distribution tight.

Our celebrity customer base has been amazingly supportive. We have a lot of loyal women who have grown with us and have charm necklaces they have been building with more charms for the past ten years. However, every day new customers are discovering us through social media, online and print platforms and now even radio. In terms of utilising social media, I think it is more about being yourself than trying to be an influencer. I watched my brand increase exponentially when I stopped being someone I am not supposed to be and I am just myself. My biggest challenge has been managing growth. It has been incredibly hard, but rewarding, to take something that I started in my bedroom and grow it into a multi-million dollar business. Having a second child has also been a challenge, but it is more about scheduling than anything. Obviously it changes things because your workload doubles, especially when you have children of two different sexes. But it's really no big deal – I have learned it's all about time management!

# *Jennifer's* ADVICE

- Don't take no for an answer.

- Be nice to everybody.

- Focus on what you should be doing and not what other people are doing.

- Reinvest your sales back into your business.

- Listen to your gut.

# MOTTO

Confidence is attractive
at any age.

# LEESA EVANS

HOLLYWOOD COSTUME DESIGNER, STYLIST

*A sought after Hollywood stylist and costume designer, Leesa Evans has dressed some of the world's biggest names. She is responsible for helping to create some of film's most iconic costumes of all time including the wardrobe of Alicia Silverstone in the film* Clueless, *the characters in* American Pie *and* Zoolander. *On the red carpet, she's dressed the likes of Rose Byrne and Amy Schumer, and is passionate about empowering female characters through costume.*

I have always loved fashion and my mother was a fashion designer when I was young, so there was endless inspiration. My imagination could just run wild. I hadn't originally planned on getting into costume design but it's been such an incredible career not only for the creative aspects, but I've so enjoyed all the travelling and amazing people I've met along the way.

The film *Clueless* was definitely a turning point for me. It was such a fun project and it's rare to have an opportunity to mix fashion and film, so I was asked to be the assistant designer because of my background and love of all things fashion. I think the yellow plaid look on Alicia Silverstone's character Cher is probably my favourite and most recognized look from the film. The experience on *Clueless* definitely inspired me to go off on my own and further pursue my career as a costume designer.

After *Clueless*, I did a few smaller films as a costume designer before landing the job on *American Pie*. At that time I was also working as a commercial stylist and private

stylist, but I had really become enamored with the process of building characters and the collaboration required in filmmaking. So it felt right to really roll up my sleeves, get to work and make it happen.

It's always a challenge to follow your dreams especially in a freelance career where there isn't a clear way to get where you want to go. But I had this thought that if I worked hard I could get there.

## THE FILMS

I never had a plan to focus so heavily on comedy. I personally love all genres of film, but there's an amazing family feel working with all the filmmakers in the Judd Apatow camp. Judd has such an incredible ability to see talent and I am continually impressed by the group he surrounds himself with: it's everyone from the cast to the crew and the creative team. It's been one of my greatest pleasures to work with so many profoundly talented women such as Kristen Wiig, Rose Byrne, Lena Dunham, Melissa McCarthy, Leslie Mann, Amy Schumer and more. I feel a sense of responsibility in helping empower their characters through clothing to fully support all aspects of the strong, intelligent, funny, beautiful women they are so they can tell an authentic story and show their dynamic complexity both on- and off-screen.

With *Zoolander*, it had always been my dream to use fashion as a character in film. The opportunity to collaborate with so many fashion designers I admire as well as design my own fashion within the *Zoolander* film was truly incredible. The original costume concept was to incorporate 50 per cent couture and 50 per cent comedy into the film and to me the perfect example is the lavender rose dress worn by Kristen Wiig's character, Alexanya.

Amy (Schumer) and I met through Judd Apatow just before *Trainwreck* and we genuinely liked each other immediately, but I could tell she wasn't a huge fan of fashion and hadn't yet found what really worked for her. So there was this exciting period of time when I got to introduce her to how good clothing can make you feel and how much fun you can have with it.

I admire Amy and her incredible talent and very generous nature – she is truly a beautiful person inside and out – so often in dressing her I want everyone to know what I know and love about her. Amy and I are both attracted to a certain simplicity in her style choices and to me it feels authentic. I know when there's an effortless tone to her look – it gives her the strength to be all that she is and all that she wants to be without having to feel self-conscious that she's trying to be someone she's not.

## MY PHILOSOPHY

My philosophy is to focus on what shapes and silhouettes make someone feel good, strong and confident. I think we all know that feeling when we feel confident in what we're wearing and the result is that you have a really great day. What if we could all have that really great day every day? I believe that confidence is more attractive than any one outfit or article of clothing and the effect of feeling so good daily is an effortlessness in getting dressed. That effortlessness makes you feel happier and then as a result kinder and that level of kindness can change the world.

My absolute favourite part of being a costume designer is coming up with the initial concept for the film. I love the fashion research, the character development, visualising the colour palette, sketching and gathering fabric swatches, making the character boards. It's the most creative moment of the film for me.

I would say my biggest success is balance and my biggest challenge has been balance. The film industry can be all encompassing and leave little time for anything else so it's been such a huge learning experience to be able to pull back time-wise to be able to do everything I want to do in life.

I am inspired by so many people for different reasons: Yves Saint Laurent for his fashion, Malala Yousafzai for her intelligence and bravery, Steve Jobs for his ingenuity, the Dalai

Lama for spreading love and the countless women inventors and activists who have paved the way for me to have so many opportunities in life.

I believe a Game Changer is someone who is committed to forging a new path creating opportunities for new perspectives. A Game Changer believes that everything is possible and embraces all challenges in achieving their dream.

**GETTING INTO THE INDUSTRY**

1. There are some amazing film and fashion schools that have costume design programs.
2. Reach out to a costume designer or stylist for an internship
3. Become a production assistant on a commercial or film shoot.
4. Contact an extras casting company to work as an extra and once you are on set before or after work go and speak to the production coordinator and convince them you are smart, resourceful and willing to work hard as a production assistant.
5. Contact someone you know who works in film or fashion and ask for an introduction to anyone hiring interns, then work hard and show them you are indispensable.

## Leesa's top 4 TIPS

- All experience is good experience.

- Work for people you admire to learn how to do things right as well as wrong.

- Fill a void in your field.

- Never give up and always be willing to look at it differently.

# MOTTO

*I realised early on that success was
tied to not giving up. Most people in this
business gave up and went on to other
things. If you simply didn't give up, you
would outlast the people who came in on
the bus with you.*

# SALLY OBERMEDER

BESTSELLING AUTHOR, TELEVISION PRESENTER, FASHION ENTREPRENEUR

*Sally Obermeder has proved to the world that some women really can have it all. Host of lifestyle television show* The Daily Edition, *bestselling author of numerous books, creator of SWIISH fashion website, cancer survivor and mum of two, Sally is the epitome of a Game Changing female – paving the path for women everywhere to follow their dreams no matter the obstacles.*

My career in journalism actually only started when I was in my late twenties. I was working in finance prior to that. It's a big switch I know! I think I always knew I wanted to work in television though. Back when I was at school, I wanted to be a newsreader but I was just way too scared to actually do it. I had heard that journalism was a 'risky' career choice – the perception was that there weren't many jobs available and pretty much no job security. So what did I do? I became an accountant instead. Close enough, right? Ha ha! It wasn't even close to my dream job but at the time I was still a bit of a finance nerd and it was a safe option. Needless to say, I really didn't enjoy it. By the time I hit my late twenties, I decided it was now or never if I was to pursue my dream of working in television. I left my job in finance and began volunteering anywhere and everywhere I could to get experience. In the beginning, there were a ton of obstacles. I didn't really know how to get work experience in TV. I decided to start out by doing a TV presenting course, which was advertised in the newspaper. While completing the course, I managed to make a few contacts who helped me get some unpaid work experience on community television (Channel 31).

During this time I really learned what it meant to work hard for what you want. I learned how to make myself an invaluable member of the team, how to network and how to go the extra mile to get the job done. Most importantly, I learned to be persistent and to never wait for others to cheer you on. Although I had a lot of good people in my life who supported my dream, there were others who didn't. They thought I was crazy! I knew if I was going to do this, I'd have to be my own cheerleader.

Eventually, I landed my first 'job' at Channel 31 – unpaid of course! But I didn't care. I was soon allowed to source, script, produce and present my own segments on a film and entertainment program called *Not The Movie Show*. This was a huge breakthrough for me and it finally felt like my hard work was beginning to pay off.

In 2005 after four years of unpaid work and internships and slogging it out, I was fortunate enough to join the Sydney Weekender team on their weekly travel and lifestyle show. This is where my career at Channel 7 began. I was there for about three years before landing a role as the National Entertainment and Lifestyle Reporter for *Today Tonight*. From there, I went on to my next (and my most recent) role as the co-host of *The Daily Edition*.

As much as I felt really ready for it when I landed the role with *Today Tonight*, it was huge in terms of the learning curve. But I was ready to give it all I had. I worked there for five years covering all the fashion, beauty, lifestyle and celebrity stories. I got to work on some incredible stories and meet some seriously interesting people. I think I did over 200 celebrity interviews in total. All with people I never could have dreamed of meeting otherwise! I had the honour of meeting and interviewing celebrities like Beyoncé, Angelina Jolie, Hugh Jackman, Mark Wahlberg, Will Ferrell and, my personal favourite, Jon Bon Jovi. I've had a crush on him forever.

The whole experience was absolutely amazing and I'm still so grateful that I was given the opportunity. It was definitely a major turning point in my career in terms of learning and growth. I learned to fight for stories in a competitive market, to pitch them, how to really hone in on what the viewer wants and create a story that's informative and entertaining. The skills that I learned at *Today Tonight* are with me and I still use them every single day at *The Daily Edition*, and I think some people would be surprised to know that those skills have absolutely and unquestionably helped us at SWIISH. I treat every blog post the same way I treated my *Today Tonight* stories.

## THE CHALLENGES

When I first found out I had cancer, there was nothing but shock. I always describe it like skipping through a field of daisies singing and laughing and then being shot from behind. You do not see it coming.

As a bit of background, I had been trying to have a baby for about six years and finally after IVF I was blessed to fall pregnant. I was beyond excited. I had the job of my dreams at Channel 7, an amazing husband and now I was finally going to have the child I had longed for. The day before she was born, I was diagnosed. It was a rare and aggressive form of breast cancer. Within a week of Annabelle coming into the world, I started intensive and aggressive chemotherapy. I was told that the cancer was Stage 3

and the prognosis and outlook was very bad. There was a slim chance of survival.

The next twelve months were an absolute nightmare. The chemo absolutely devastated my body. It was so severe that my skin turned yellow, my nails fell off, my mouth filled with ulcers and my throat burned. I remember howling in pain as I tried to fall asleep. Painkillers were no use. They fought against the chemo drugs and I felt as though I had no relief. I just cried and cried.

All this time, I had a newborn baby to raise. I didn't even know if I was going to live to see her grow up. I wondered every day how I could pass on to Annabelle everything I wanted her to know, everything that I would want to share and teach her at every age.

I struggled to find the strength to keep on going. Some days, I felt as though it would be so much easier to just give up. But then I thought about Annabelle. I refused to accept that I wouldn't be around for her. So I dug deep and found the fighter within me. I said 'game on mole' to the cancer – it was the enemy and this was war.

Writing the book *Never Stop Believing* was incredibly difficult, but it was something I knew I needed to do. I wanted to do it because I hoped it would help other people who were in the same position as me. It's not easy putting your whole life out in the open, especially when it comes to something like cancer. It's scary, it's raw and it's very personal. But I hoped that by sharing my story, someone out there would feel less alone in their own battle.

Although I do talk about cancer in detail, *Never Stop Believing* shares my entire life story. In the book, I also talk about throwing away a safe, steady job and financial security in order to chase my dream career, as well as the struggles I faced trying to have a baby. Of course, it was difficult at times to revisit some of the darker moments but I knew I had to include them. I knew that if I was going to write this book, I couldn't skip over the gritty details. It had to be honest and from the heart.

More than five years on I still get emails and letters from readers. For many, the book gave them a ray of hope when times were rough, while others simply found comfort knowing that they were not alone in their experience. This is exactly why I wrote the book in the first place and it makes it all worthwhile.

## SWIISH AND SMOOTHIES

After I wrote *Never Stop Believing*, I was determined to continue staying focused on my recovery back to health – which included drinking Super Green Smoothies every day. I got back into fitness as well and I began to look and feel better than ever before. I really felt as though I was getting my life back.

I was also determined to keep pushing forward in my career. This was around the time that I landed my job as the co-host of *The Daily Edition*, which I was over the moon about. In addition to that, I was working hard to expand our business – SWIISH.com

SWIISH first came about while I was still recovering from my first surgery. I was literally in my hospital bed when I came up with the idea of doing a blog that focused on luxe for less. I've always believed that we shouldn't have to choose between living a fabulous lifestyle and saving money. A luxe for less blog seemed like the perfect idea.

I remember immediately ringing Maha (my sister and SWIISH co-founder) excitedly suggesting that we do it. She also had a suggestion – that I concentrate on my treatment. Ha ha ha! She was right, but as soon as I was at the end of my treatment, we jumped into action.

The first thing we had to do was come up with a name. It took us a few goes, but eventually we came up with SWIISH. It stands for Stylish Women Inspiring Inner Strength, Health and Happiness. Maha and I just really wanted a name that would describe who we wanted to be, who we wanted our readers to be and what we wanted to achieve all at the same time. SWIISH also made us think of the swish of a skirt when you walk, or a swish of lipstick, or the swish of an email being sent as deals got done.
It was all about a strong woman in today's dynamic world.

Then came the hard part… actually putting together the blog! This wasn't just some little side project. We worked around the clock, spending all our free time designing the website, writing blog posts and developing graphics. I still remember taking photos with a clunky old camera and learning about this Instagram thing that had just hit the market.

I won't lie, there were plenty of days when we wondered what the hell we were doing. For anyone who has started a business, you will know what I mean. There's no off button. Many days, you're the receptionist, the accountant, the creative director, the shopkeeper, the writer, the therapist and the CEO all in one. It didn't matter though because we were so determined. We knew what we wanted and we persevered. Five years on and we couldn't be more thrilled, humbled and excited by how incredibly well the site has been received by our readers.

I don't think Maha and I ever knew SWIISH was going to be a success. Although there were a few key moments that really helped to get us off the ground. One of those was Super Green Smoothies. When we realised all the wonders these smoothies were doing for our bodies (and how good we were getting at making them!) we knew people would be interested. When the book *Super Green Smoothies* came out, it was an instant hit but at the same time it helped to draw even more people to the site.

The second point when we realised SWIISH was going to have success was in

2015. It was the year we launched our online store. It started off with just a handful of fashion and homewares, along with our books, but it quickly started to grow. Our readers immediately jumped on board and started ordering.

Customers loved our products, as they reflected the luxe for less mantra of the blog. We got a lot of newcomers to our site and store through word of mouth, and the power of social media. People wanted to be in the know about what new products were coming out – whether it was fashion, accessories, beauty products, homewares or our books and 30 Day Challenges.

Recently everyone has become obsessed with our Super Green Superfood Powder – we can barely keep up with the demand, which we are so grateful for. Knowing that we are in some way helping people feel good from the inside out just makes Maha and me feel so happy, and it's hugely fulfilling.

Back to the smoothies. When I first found out about Super Green Smoothies I was still in my cancer recovery. I had put on over fifteen kilograms of baby weight and chemo weight and my body had been really badly battered by the chemo. I'd heard about green smoothies before and the wonders they could do for your body, but I honestly thought they would taste horrible.

But then when I started making them myself, I realised they could actually be pretty delicious. It wasn't long until I had Maha drinking them too and that's when the recipe testing started. We were always in the kitchen, mixing up ingredients, making new combos and swapping them with each other. Throughout the process, we both ended up losing a ton of weight. I felt so lean, my hair and nails grew back stronger and my skin got its glow back. We were both bouncing with energy and Maha was sleeping better too. People kept saying things like 'What have you guys been doing? You look amazing!' And that's when we realised that sharing our recipes might be a good idea. We started writing them down and fine-tuning them to make sure they had maximum taste and nutrition. We then finally decided to put them altogether into our very own recipe book – *Super Green Smoothies*.

Then came the hard part – trying to get it published. You'd think that with years of experience in TV and a published book already under my belt, it would be easy to get *Super Green Smoothies* out. Unfortunately, it didn't go quite that smoothly. I remember calling my publisher with the idea and they straight up said, 'We don't think anyone will buy it.' Another publisher replied with, 'Who is going to drink those things? If anything, it will be a fad that won't last'.

Eventually Maha and I decided to self-publish the ebook. We wrote it at home, took all the pictures ourselves in our kitchen and slaved away until we were happy with it. It came out in September 2014 and shot up the iTunes charts, hitting number one within the first couple of days. It also hit a bunch of number 1 lists on Amazon. This is when we got the call from the publishers to say that they had perhaps been a little hasty in turning it down, and they wanted to publish the book.

From there, we started working with them on the paperback version, which we released in April 2015. It hit number one right away and we are so incredibly proud to say that it's now in its eleventh reprint! It finished the year as the number three non-fiction book in Australia, and it is still Australia's number one smoothie book. It's also been reprinted in Poland!

The most rewarding part, though, is all the emails we receive from people in Australia and across the world, including France, the US, the UK, Ireland, even Iceland. They tell us how their skin is glowing, their hair and nails are stronger, they've lost weight, they're sleeping better and they have so much more energy. It's amazing to hear how Super Green Smoothies have helped people to transform their health and their lives. It definitely makes it all worth it!

## THE BRAND

Our brand does seem to be constantly getting bigger and bigger. We're so grateful to have reached a stage where we can expand and think about new products.

The idea for the Super Green Smoothies frozen packs came around three years ago. It was right after Maha and I had gone shopping for our smoothie ingredients. I remember lugging the kale, the spinach and pineapple back from the shops, wishing that someone would do all the smoothie prep for me. I didn't feel like prepping – I just wanted to sit on the couch and read magazines. Ha ha! I said to Maha, 'I wish there was someone to prep my smoothie for me.' She laughed at me but at the same time, she knew I was serious.

Maha and I quickly realised that we weren't the only ones who felt this way. So many people who loved drinking the smoothies kept getting in touch with us and saying, 'I have no time to prep! How can I make my smoothies faster?' and, 'I'm always in a rush in the morning, can I make my smoothies the night before?' That cemented it for us – it was time to take this Super Green Smoothies obsession of ours to the next level. We had to make it faster, easier and more accessible.

We partnered with a manufacturer who specialises in frozen foods, and started figuring out which recipes we wanted to include, and how we could make them as quick, easy and affordable as possible. Our main aim was to create a product that had all the taste and benefits with none of the waste that comes with preparing your own smoothie (you know, wilted herbs and veggies in the bottom of the fridge!). As you can imagine, there was a lot of trial and error but eventually we nailed it. After we got those tricky parts out of the way, we got to work on the fun stuff like the package design. Then came the daunting part – trying to get the product into supermarkets. We had a 'meeting' with the product buyers at Coles and Woolies. I say 'meeting' because that's technically what it is, but that's not what it feels like. In fact, it feels more like an episode of *Shark Tank* than anything else. Ha ha!

It really is such a nerve-wracking process! Often, they'll tell you what you need to change before they'd consider the product. You can then come back with the updated version and try again. Luckily for us, they loved the product from the get-go. We had already anticipated many of their questions, in particular around the size of the packs, and had factored this into the design. Maha and I were over the moon when both Coles and Woolworths agreed to stock our Super Green Smoothies in all stores across Australia. Seeing them on the shelf for the first time was a huge 'pinch me' moment! We are beyond excited about this. For three years we've laboured away on this passion project and to see it now come to life is a dream come true.

## BACK TO TELEVISION

When I landed the role as the co-host of *The Daily Edition*, I had already been working at Channel 7 for a number of years. I felt like moving into a co-hosting role was the next natural progression for me. I had to do test screenings alongside my other co-hosts, to make sure that the chemistry was there.

I've been there for over three years now and every day is such a buzz. I get to co-host alongside Tom Williams, whom I adore. We cover news and lifestyle and I love it. I truly couldn't enjoy it more. I'm on maternity leave at the moment but I am missing it!

When I'm at work and not on maternity leave, I can't say that I have any 'typical' days. I usually try to get up early, so I can get a bit of a workout in before I started my day. It would usually either be a walk or an F45 class. I then come home and make brekkie (a Super Green Smoothie) and get Annabelle ready for her day. (I imagine it'll be a bit different now when I go back to work now that I have two kids to get sorted!) I head into SWIISH to either check online content or meet with buyers for the online store or we might have a quick photo shoot. I then have to head to Channel 7 so I could be in studio before midday to do voice-overs, read over scripts and have a pre-production meeting. Then the show will begin!

The thing I love about *The Daily Edition* is that there's such a good mix of stories. There's breaking news, inspiring stories of everyday people and mix of pop culture thrown in. No two days are the same and the greatest privilege is that we are exposed to so much.

## THE FUTURE

Before I got sick, I always pictured I would have two or even three children. After Annabelle was born, I just felt so lucky to have one healthy baby. I wasn't thinking about having another child then. I didn't even know if I was going to survive long enough to see Annabelle turn one year old, let alone to have another baby. My focus was solely on getting better so that I could give Annabelle the childhood she deserved. Once I was finally given the all clear from my cancer, Marcus and I decided we wanted to give Annabelle a little brother or sister.

A few years later, I began talking to my doctor about having another baby. We still had embroyos remaining from when Annabelle was conceived via IVF. Unfortunately, I was told in no uncertain terms that it's far too dangerous for me to carry a child again, in terms of the cancer returning. I was absolutely heartbroken. I knew that I was extremely lucky to have one child, but the yearning and desire to be a mum again was so strong. I wasn't going to put myself at risk of getting cancer again though. I couldn't do that to my family.

It was then that Marcus and I began considering surrogacy. There are so many things to consider when it comes to surrogacy, not just the laws but everything – the lengthy process, the distance between you and your child if your surrogate is overseas, plus the emotional side of it. In some cases, financial burden can become a huge issue as well. In Australia, paying a surrogate is considered a criminal offence. At the same time, it's not easy to find a woman who is willing to do it for free (altruistic surrogacy). Australia just isn't set up for it as much as over-seas. I didn't know anyone who could be an altruistic surrogate, so we looked to the US. This is where we found our miracle – Rachel.

Rachel is one of the most beautiful people I have ever met. She's warm, caring and funny, she's an amazing mother and she lives to help other people. After hearing my story, Rachel was willing to have our baby for us and asked for nothing in return. Words could not describe how grateful we felt. It was like a ray of hope had finally come back into our lives. Although Rachel started IVF as soon as possible, the journey ended up being longer and more emotional than we thought.

I still remember the day when the doctor gave Rachel and I the incredible news. The IVF had worked and Rachel was pregnant. I was overwhelmed with emotion and excitement. It had been an extremely tough journey. After years, two failed pregnancies and one miscarriage, Marcus and I were finally going to have the child we had yearned for. Annabelle was going to have a sibling.

I am super busy, but I wouldn't give up any of it! This year, I actually told myself I wasn't going to take on anything else too big. Then again, I told myself the same thing about a year ago and look where I am now… I have a new baby, a new Super Green Superfood Powder, Super Green Smoothies in the supermarket and another book on the way! I guess I just thrive off having something new and innovative to work on. I constantly have ideas about what our next big thing is going to be, how I'm going to change this or improve that. Sometimes I have to stop myself though and realise that I can't actually do a thousand things at once. Ha ha!

In all seriousness though, I don't have any more 'big' plans at the moment. I'm just enjoying my maternity leave and time with my family. Everything is going fabulously at SWIISH. Maha and I have a great team, our customers are happy, our products are flying out the door and our new Super Green Smoothies freezer packs are going gangbusters.

We definitely have plans to revamp the website with a fresh new look and expand our love for our community through some new sections on our site, including one called 'Like A

Boss' where we showcase new businesses and give them some publicity, as we know how hard it is to get the word out when you're just starting your business.

At the end of the day though, Elyssa is so little and Annabelle has just started school, so I'm relishing my mum duties. These are important years and they'll be gone before I know it. I don't want to miss a thing!

## THE INSPIRATION

I wouldn't really say I have one mentor. I basically just adopted the mantra early on that you can learn something from everyone. As a result, I try to be really present when I'm in a new environment and pay attention – like a sponge soaking up as much knowledge as possible. If I need advice, the first person I will turn to is either Marcus or Maha. Throughout my career, I've been given the most amazing opportunities to work with some of the best and brightest. Sarah Stinson, our Executive Producer for *The Daily Edition*, who I also worked with on *Today Tonight*, has been incredible to work with. Larry Emdur has always been another go-to when I need someone to bounce ideas off.

The most important thing I would say to aspiring entrepreneurs is that you have to be prepared. What I mean by that is you have to be prepared to do whatever it takes to follow your dream. I worked unpaid for many years. I'm not saying it will be the same for everyone, but if that's what it takes, then you have to be willing to do that. Don't listen to the naysayers (and there can be many) who tell you your idea sucks or your business won't succeed. Believe in what you're doing, and persist. Never give up.

## BEING A GAME CHANGER

I think being a Game Changer can mean a lot of things to different people but, for me, it's all about having the power to change your own life. I think that a lot of people choose a life path early on and think they have to stick with it. They think 'this is just the way it is' and they just go through the motions. I'll admit, I was the same at one stage! Until one day I decided that enough was enough. I realised that the only person who had control over my life was me. If I wanted a different path for myself, I was going to have to blaze one myself. So I did!

Today, being a Game Changer for me is about always pushing the boundaries. It's about being true to yourself and fearlessly following your passions. I'm always looking for ways to challenge myself and the word 'can't' isn't a word I use a lot. If I have an idea and I believe in it strongly enough, I'll find a way to make it happen.

# Sally's
# ADVICE

- Ask for help when you need it! As women, we naturally look after others so it can be hard to take a step back and say, 'Please help me.' For me, it was saying, 'Can someone please watch Annabelle after I've put her to bed so Marcus and I can walk around the corner and have dinner together?'

- Have good organisation systems in place at home. For example, when it comes to cooking, I take shortcuts where I can. I'm always cooking extra when I make home cooked meals (as long as it's stuff that can freeze well). I also used to pre-prep all my smoothie ingredients and keep them in zip lock bags in the freezer. Now I tend to just use our Super Green Smoothie frozen packs. They save so much time!

- Give yourself a break in motherhood! Remember, there's no right way to do anything when it comes to raising children. It's all about what works best for you and your child and your family. Don't beat yourself up about it! At the end of the day what matters is how much you love them and making sure they know that you value their mental, emotional and physical health and safety above anything else.

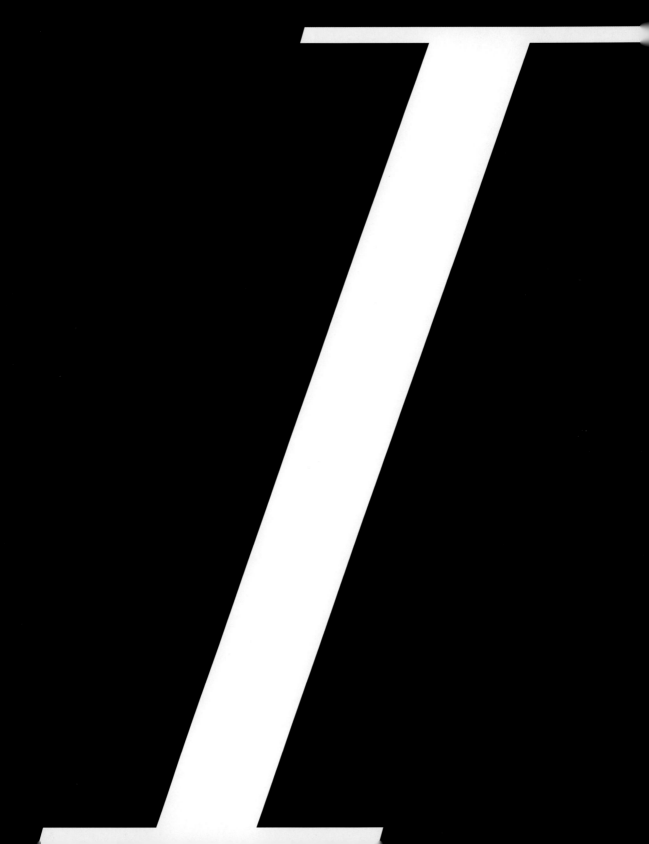

*I NEVER DREAMED ABOUT SUCCESS, I WORKED FOR IT*

**ESTÉE LAUDER**

# MOTTO

*The only person you are destined to*
*become is the person you decide to be.*

# CANDICE LAKE

STYLE EDITOR, MODEL, PHOTOGRAPHER, BLOGGER

*Candice Lake is an Australian-born photographer, blogger and model. Her fashion label Candidate by Candice Lake was named on US* Vogue's *best dressed list. She is TRESemmé's Global Brand Ambassador and is the Contributing Style Editor at* Vogue Australia.

I had always wanted to go to art school when I was younger although somehow I ended up at law school. A couple of years into it, I luckily fell into modelling and everything else went out the window. I met the most extraordinary people and experienced things I never would have had access to without modelling. It was an accelerated life lesson and it was a few years into it that, while in between shots on a shoot for *Harpers Bazaar*, I asked the photographer if I could possibly come with him on his next shoot to assist. That was how I began assisting fashion photographers and transitioned to the other side of the camera while gaining a Fine Arts Bachelor degree. Without modelling, I would never have had these amazing opportunities in photography.

I think that it is an exciting time to be a creative person and to have your own brand.

Now more than ever, with the movement of young entrepreneurs and the democratisation of the industry through social media and online accessibility, you can be a photographer, model, blogger, entrepreneur, designer and creative director all under the umbrella of one brand, which is most exciting.

My biggest challenge has been having a child and wanting to really stop and enjoy the precious and limited time with him, in the middle of building a brand. I found it very conflicting personally and professionally, trying to balance the two. I travelled with my son everywhere so we were never separated in his first year, and I only took on jobs that were really important to me. It ended up being a really positive experience and made me really assess my direction although, at the time, it was quite difficult. Now, my main aim is that whatever I am putting my energy into, I am giving it 100 per cent. Once I accepted it was about quality and not quantity of time, our life was a lot richer and my business flourished.

I learned pretty early on that nothing just falls into your lap. You have to make it happen and take advantage of any opportunities you've been given. I work extremely hard to make sure I am pushing myself to produce the best quality of work on every single job I do. I didn't just wake up one day and

# Candice's
# *TIPS*

- Always do what you're afraid to do. If something seems easy, you're not pushing yourself hard enough.

- Listen to your gut instinct, take risks, don't take no for an answer and work your butt off doing something you love.

suddenly shoot for big brands. I hustled, I worked for free for a *long* time, I carried sand-bags up and down and then back up sand dunes for photographers, and learned to not take no for an answer. I learned to listen to my gut instinct despite everyone's doubts. When people told me modelling was a waste of time, I knew it would allow me to see the world. And then later when everyone told me I was insane to quit modelling to go back to art school, I knew it was right.

I don't really have any major regrets, I really believe that if even if you fail once, twice or a hundred times, you are still moving forward. I believe in learning from all mistakes you make along the way to create more opportunities. If you always act with integrity, you should have no regrets.

Angela Ahrendts has definitely been a big inspiration. I love that she was a pioneer of embracing the digital world and, against all odds, she turned Burberry around from an ageing British icon into one of the fastest growing global luxury brands in the world. Also my husband – he has such a beautiful mind and is an incredibly talented architect and visionary. He is constantly inspiring and pushing me creatively. It is a real joy to share your life with someone whom you admire greatly.

# MOTTO

*Anything is possible and never, never, never give up.*

# LORNA JANE CLARKSON

FOUNDER OF LORNA JANE ACTIVEWEAR, CREATOR OF ACTIVE LIVING

*Lorna Jane revolutionised women's fitness clothing more than twenty-seven years ago, founding Lorna Jane. She creates functional and feminine designs, is passionate about active living and now has more than 200 stores globally.*

Before I started the business, I was working as a dental therapist during the day and teaching fitness classes after work and on weekends. When I started designing activewear, it was never my plan to build a brand, let alone an entire category. I was simply designing clothes that I could work out in, but that I could also wear throughout the day. I wanted them to look good and feel comfortable at the same time.

I discovered that, while designing clothes to fit my busy lifestyle, so many women felt the same – and those women became my customers. When I started designing workout wear, everything women wore to work out in was totally 'sport specific'. So when you went running, you wore your 'running gear', and when you were doing yoga, you wore your 'yoga pants' and so on. I wanted to create clothing that you could not only wear to work out in, but could be worn from morning to night and would actually inspire you to be more active in your daily life. Today, women are busier than ever and they wear their activewear *everywhere* – which is exactly what I predicted and a dream come true for me.

I've built my business from the ground up and over the past twenty-seven years there have been so many amazing moments and achievements – but just as many challenges. Facing challenges, making mistakes and taking chances is what building a business is all about. I've learned that you have to be comfortable being outside your comfort zone, because change and adaptation is what keeps your business moving forward and your products relevant in the marketplace.

I think the biggest challenge in business and in life is to stay focused on your goals and not be swayed by naysayers or popular opinion. Obviously, it's important to have feedback and input from other people on your team or in your life, but it's also important to trust your own instincts and intuition and to remember that this is ultimately your vision and your dream, and you and only you are the one who is going to make it happen.

## THE SUCCESS OF LORNA JANE

There are so many things that determine a brand's success but I think with Lorna Jane the most significant aspect would have to be that we represent so much more than our products. Lorna Jane and our Active Living philosophy inspires women all over the world to recognise the importance of investing in their health and wellness. We give them the inspiration, the tools and the products to be active every day and we are rewarded with their support and loyalty to the brand.

When you build a brand, it helps when it's a true reflection of who you are and what you believe in. I love fashion, am obsessed with health and fitness and am an eternal optimist. This is who I am and what my brand has become and it is this that ultimately allows us to be authentic and lead the way in the activewear category.

# *Lorna's* TIPS

- Find what it is that you love to do and work out a way to turn it into a business.

- Be careful who you choose to walk beside you – work only with people who are like-minded and share your vision for your brand.

- Know that nothing worthwhile was built overnight – you will be challenged, you will question why you should keep going and you will be misunderstood. However, remember that this is when you need to remind yourself why you started in the first place.

- Push through because it is usually after the hardest of times that you actually see progress.

# MOTTO

'Stay hungry, stay foolish.' I am always motivated to keep learning and developing myself, I believe this is a very important factor in everything you do. Steve Jobs has been an inspiration for me, from the beginning to everything I am doing right now.

# NEGIN MIRSALEHI

INFLUENCER, BEAUTY ENTREPRENEUR, CREATOR OF GISOU

*Negin Mirsalehi is a fashion and beauty blogger, boasting a social media following of more than four million people. She is the creator of hair care brand Gisou, which is made from pure honey inspired by her father's bee garden and her love of bees.*

Growing up I never knew specifically what I wanted to do as a job and this was still an issue for me until I graduated from university. My journey as an online influencer started three to four years ago, when I was still a full-time student at the University of Amsterdam. I was writing my thesis when a friend of mine recommended to start with Instagram. It was on Instagram that I became familiar with various bloggers and became curious about what the blogging phenomena really entailed. After some research and seeing what it was all about, I realised that this was something that was made for me. I did not start like most bloggers did ten years ago who started posting pictures, which turned into being their full-time job. The journey I had was more planned, becoming a big worldwide blogger and making it my career was really one of my purposes. But I did not expect my blog and Instagram to blow up so fast, into something so big.

When I started my own website a few years ago, I would only post blogs about my personal fashion taste. Because social media has become so popular, I only use those platforms now to do that. My website's purpose is to inspire my followers with stories. When I started on Instagram my main goal was to inspire, pretty much the same as it is now. But back then I was still studying so I had to combine both work and study. After finishing my studies I was so happy that I could completely focus on my passion. I really feel that focus is very important when it comes to chasing your dreams.

## BUILDING A FOLLOWING

My followers started to increase quite rapidly. I always aimed for collaborations with brands such as Louis Vuitton, Dolce & Gabbana, Dior and more. To achieve this you have to put yourself on the map. Who are you and do you do? Do you take your job seriously? Is there a connection? It took some time to get there, but I am very proud of all the collaborations I have done so far.

At the beginning I only shared my outfits of the day on Instagram. At a certain point I realised I wanted to share more of what I do, so I started to post more personal things like my beauty routine and the food I ate, but also stuff pertaining to my education, my family and our love of bees. Since I decided to do that, I've noticed that I've attracted more people and that my interaction has greatly increased. I guess that's the result of people feeling as though they know me better on a more personal and intimate level. It's clear that the more personal things you share, the more people will connect to you and like it. That's why YouTubers who make vlogs have huge followings. For me, I only share the things I feel comfortable with. I will never share everything.

## CREATING A BRAND

Before I decided to start my Instagram account, I had created a clear vision and plan for it and this helped me a lot. From day one I knew I wanted to focus on creating high quality content with a cosmopolitan character. The story began with my father, who is a beekeeper, and my mother, who is a hairdresser. Some of my fondest childhood memories stem from growing up in the bee garden. It was my playground and a place filled with only positive vibes, laughter and lots of love.

## THE EVOLUTION OF GISOU

Gisou was born naturally out of my passion for bees, the bee garden and beauty. You could say beekeeping has always been in my blood. My father learned it from his father, who was taught by my great-grandfather and so on. When moving to the Netherlands, my mother started experimenting with her own hair care solutions. One thing my mother knew for sure was that my dad's honey was going to be the key ingredient. Now I have the opportunity to combine my love for family and beauty into the brand Gisou.

Four years ago, when I started on Instagram with inspirational fashion posts, I acknowledged that a lot of people were interested in my hair. After receiving so many

questions about my hair, I felt like I had something to offer and I decided to share the healing powers of bee products. This resulted in Gisou: a bee based hair product line. I knew that the story was of a special nature, however, I never thought that people would be interested in bees or the bee story behind the brand. I definitely believe that people can resonate with the story as it is very authentic and real. I try to share my personal story via my Instagram account and YouTube channel, where my followers can see me work in my father's bee garden or my moments with my mom when she is doing my hair.

## THE FUTURE

We are currently working very hard on more hair care products for Gisou. I am so proud to be able to expand this line, as it is something that is so dear to me. It includes my family and my most cherished childhood memories in the Mirsalehi bee garden. We are currently busy with expanding our Gisou hair product line, so exciting things are happening!

We have launched two hair products, both containing ingredients produced by honey-bees. The Gisou Honey Infused Hair Oil is an exclusive hair oil enriched with honey from my dad's bee garden. With help from my mum, we were able to use the healing power of honey to create a multi-purpose hair oil. The Gisou Propolis Heat Protecting Spray protects hair from damage caused by the heat of blow dryers, styling tools and the sun.We are working hard on new products and formulas, so stay tuned for some new Gisou!

## THE IMPORTANCE OF SOCIAL MEDIA

I have a very solid follower base, which makes them potential Gisou customers. My followers trust me in some sort of way and consider me as an influencer. They were open to trying my product because of their interest in my hair. Even though they trust me and Gisou, the products we offer have to be of good quality in order for them to become loyal customers. I believe that quality is the key ingredient of Gisou as I always try to find the best formulas, for example, the formulas that my mother created for the Honey Infused Hair Oil that work so extremely well.

Whether it is about Gisou or the collaborations that I take on with brands, I always take time to think about my ideas and the proper way to execute them. The beauty industry is very diverse
and I believe that what makes Gisou so special is that I launched a bee-based hair care line that not only delivers quality but also the story of the Mirsalehi bees and my personal story.

When I started my Instagram account I worked day and night to make it into something that would inspire others. Currently, I am always thinking of new ideas to keep inspiring my followers. When I created my brand, Gisou, it was of great importance that we made sure that the brand would also stand out on social media and inspire women to take care of their hair. I believe

that healthy hair is beautiful hair and with Gisou I want to share this message. In this day and age it is is important to adapt your marketing strategy to your target group, thus social media is definitely a key aspect in our strategy. We see that satisfied customers share their purchases online and we continuously get tagged in pictures of happy customers on the Gisou Instagram page @gisou_official. This makes it very real for us, having customers who share their experience online and would like to be associated with Gisou. I also like to share images of loyal customers through my social media channels.

## THE IMPORTANCE OF PASSION

I believe that success starts with passion. I was lucky enough to find my passion during my study in Business Administration and Marketing. But without perseverance and dedication I would have never been where I am at the moment. Strive for your goals no matter what and surround yourself with people who support you in this. Planning and market research can be essential before you start something. My recipe for success is to work very hard and to never forget the reason why I started, which is my passion for fashion, beauty and lifestyle. Also, it helps a lot to surround myself with positive people that get our work spirit. I also feel very lucky to have my boyfriend as my business part-ner because we have the same goals and he's the best when it comes to handling the business side. Lastly, I really feel that focus is very important when it comes to chasing your dreams.

## *Negin's top* 3 *TIPS*

- My most important advice is to do research and see how you can do things differently. Now-adays I feel like a lot of girls create mind-blowing content. But with only that, chances are that you won't be able to turn your passion into your profession.

- Try to see what it takes to make it work; think about your reach and how different social platforms can benefit that.

- Always keep your eyes open for new platforms.

*WHATEVER YOU WANT IN LIFE, OTHER PEOPLE ARE GOING TO WANT IT TOO. BELIEVE IN YOURSELF ENOUGH TO ACCEPT THE IDEA THAT YOU HAVE AN EQUAL RIGHT TO IT*

**DIANE SAWYER**

# MOTTO

Trust your instincts.

# BECKY COOPER & BRIDGET YORSTON

## FASHION DESIGNERS

*Becky Cooper and Bridget Yorston are the eclectic designers behind Bec & Bridge, the exciting Australian label worn by the likes of Kim Kardashian West and Gigi Hadid. Born out of a friendship between the girls while studying together at university, the brand has boomed into an international phenomenon.*

"We met on our first day of studying fashion design at the University of Technology in Sydney. We did everything together and were basically inseparable. We never really set out to start a label, it all just happened very organically. In our second year of university a friend asked us to revamp an old pair of his jeans. From there, more friends wanted us to revamp their jeans and before we knew it we had received an order for 200 pairs of jeans from a prominent store. The brand Bec & Bridge was born and evolved from there.

We were so young when it all started and with youth comes resilience. The hours were long and we made no money but we loved what we did! We had to learn and understand every aspect of the business. We made so many mistakes but they were also important lessons. The sales started slowly but iconic retailers like Bracewell, Tuchuzy and David Jones definitely helped garner brand recognition.

When we graduated from UTS we won the Australian Business Limited award. This was a cash prize as well as business support. We were also invited to participate in the New Generation show at Australian Fashion Week. Both helped us realise that this was the right path and next step for our brand. Getting picked up by David Jones back in 2006 was a big 'pinch me' moment. David Jones is such an iconic department store to be associated with from a brand and business point of view and it really helped to take Bec & Bridge to the next level. We are so fortunate that they have supported the Bec & Bridge brand continuously for so many years and it' s been really exciting to see our brand grow within their stores.

The Bec & Bridge girl that inspires us has a modern femininity about her. We always look to the raw and healthy supermodels of the 70s and 90s for inspiration and this comes through in each collection. The brand prides itself on delivering collections that offer a combination of aspirational and seasonal must-have pieces.

## THE FOLLOWING

Miranda Kerr was definitely one of the first big names. At the time, Miranda was the ambassador for David Jones. She chose to wear one of our dresses at the season launch. We couldn't quite believe the response. The dress sold out almost immediately. We have been really fortunate and feel really honoured to have had such amazing support from stylists, influencers and celebrities globally. While we love dressing some of the world's biggest celebrity names, we also love to dress the cool young up and comers. Some of our favourite Bec & Bridge girls that we've dressed are Kim Kardashian West, Bella Hadid, Gigi Hadid, Hailey Baldwin, Kendall Jenner, Taylor Swift, Emily Ratajkowski and Chrissy Teigen. More recently we have dressed musicians Lion Babe and Jhené Aiko who we are big fans of.

Watching the brand expand globally has been incredibly humbling. Social media is an incredibly important tool for our brand. It speaks directly to our customer and we use it on a daily basis. We use apps such as Instagram to showcase our campaigns and let our customers know when collections have launched in stores and online. We have a close relationship with a lot of the Australian and international influencers and celebrities who we absolutely adore. They have been so supportive over the years and have definitely played a significant role in brand exposure and growth. We have also worked with a few influencers and musicians, such as Jesse Jo Stark, Natasha Oakley and Nadia Fairfax on digital and campaign shoots and exclusive capsule collections and this is something we will continue to do. Next for Bec & Bridge? 2017 is a big year for us as we open the doors to our first retail store in Sydney. Our goal is for a few more retail stores to follow.

# *Bec & Bridge's* TIPS

- Know your strengths and weaknesses.

- Trust your instincts.

- Learn from your mistakes.

- Exercise patience.

# MOTTO

*True passion is what matters.*

# KRISTINA BAZAN

SOCIAL INFLUENCER, CREATOR OF KAYTURE

*Kristina Bazan is wise beyond her years. She launched her fashion and beauty blog, Kayture, five years ago and has already amassed more than two million followers, is a L'Oréal Paris Brand Ambassador, has been featured in* Forbes 30 Under 30 *and has appeared on the cover of* Vogue Portugal. *She has forayed into music and even written a book* On the Go, *all in her early twenties.*

I was seventeen years old and still in high school when I realised creativity was in my bones and that I had always wanted to do so many different things with my life, and what a better time to start! I had a boyfriend who was in photography and he started taking editorial photos of me. We sent out some of the pictures to an agent who convinced us that we should keep going.

LOOKBOOK.nu was a popular social media platform at the time. I began using it, posting my 'photos of the day' and started getting a lot of traction. At the time I was living in a tiny village in Switzerland where the average age is sixty years old. I had cows and goats in the front of my house. There was one bus every hour. It was kind of miserable and boring. So all of a sudden, being able to have a hobby was really fun for me. Six months after posting photos, somehow *Vogue* heard about me, my photos and what James and I were doing. I got invited to an event in Tokyo where I realised that there was a lot of potential in what we were doing. So James put together a business plan with the aim of creating a company.

Honestly, my first goal was to be able to sustain myself – and also convince my parents to not make me go to college! It is a scary thing to dive into the blue, and we definitely needed something consistent.

**BUILDING THE BRAND**

Our business plan was pretty simple: to create editorials that you would see in the likes of *Vogue* magazine. After all, French *Vogue* was my bible. But it always seemed extremely unrelatable – no girl can technically afford the outfits featured in the pages and so I always managed to find stuff at Zara or vintage items and make it look like it was in a magazine through styling. Our plan was to basically make editorials – just James and I. We focused on creating iconic, beautiful images with the aim of inspiring a large community of people. We had no makeup artist, no lighting, no fancy sets – just images that we hoped would be more relatable to the women who started to follow us. It seemed to work because big brands got interested in us super quickly, while so many women started wanting to shop for the stuff I was wearing. The brand grew organically – we kept producing images, and the followers

*Kristina's* TIPS

- Always create topnotch quality posts.

- Have an artist's concept.

- Try to target the right people.

- Be aware of who you're talking to.

kept on coming. The interest just grew and grew.

The social media landscape is changing so quickly, and it's kind of scary! I focused on being innovative – not so much on growing my followers, but rather on creating quality content because that is what is going to last.

Of course it is good to have a lot of followers, but it is better to inspire a conversation and engage with the readers. The motto that I stick by is that every post needs to be topnotch quality.

There is a lot of speculation about how we make money and whether we just post anything for the sake of it. But that is not true. For me, the most important thing I have learned is to be very picky in regards to my projects. My main income comes from choosing the right partners and creating long term projects.

L'Oréal is one of the main ones right now and we now have about 10-15 partners that we do regular projects with, rather than saying yes to everything. It gives us a certain power – to be able to choose what we want to accept. This also allows me to say no to a lot of things. Of course when you have salaries to pay and a team to look after, you have to make sure you have enough cashflow!

One of my favourite projects to work on has been with Mugler as they allowed me to art direct the whole thing. I created the whole video concept for three different fragrances with my best friend. I even got to write a song for it and did a huge promotion on my end. They trusted me so much on everything and that is what I love – working with incredible brands on big projects that become bigger than social media and blog posts. At the moment it's important for me to evolve and establish myself more and more, not just throughout my blog, but outside social media. I'm extremely passionate about art directing outside the blog, working for brands and magazines, and creating editorials. Music is also a big part of my time. I am putting together new music for my album, which I am super passionate about and want to let grow organically.

Several years ago, when I was still living in Switzerland, I had a French editor reach out to me asking me to share my stuff with an international audience, which is how my first book came about, *On The Go*. It was a lot of fun putting together and something I am very proud of.

## HOW TO BE A SOCIAL INFLUENCER

Try to emulate your own success and figure out what you're good at. I think we all have something very special to share, and it's important to figure out what it is and try to make a good impact. I'm still figuring out what I want my impact to be but I definitely don't want to confine myself to only blogging, I think it's almost too shallow at times. I want to use my influence and voice to spread a message on work ethic and to encourage young women to create their own system; to inspire women (and men as well) to pursue their passions even if they have social pressures from family and friends to do something else. I am grateful to do something of my own, and it's good to be reminded that no matter what you do, true passion is what matters.

*IF YOU
DON'T LIKE
THE ROAD
YOU ARE WALKING
START PAVING
ANOTHER ONE*

DOLLY PARTON

# MOTTO

Be who you are. My mission is
to empower women to feel good
about themselves. That's my vision
of beauty and it's different from all
the other cosmetic companies.

# BOBBI BROWN

FOUNDER OF BOBBI BROWN COSMETICS

*Bobbi Brown is the name and brains behind one of the top cosmetic brands in the world. The makeup artist started with a simple idea and her brand is now sold in more than seventy countries worldwide. She is a champion for women's rights and passionate about female empowerment through education. She volunteers for a number of charities and believes strongly in giving back.*

Makeup has always been my passion. It started when I was five years old and got into my mother's makeup drawer – I began playing with her makeup, applying it to my face, the sink and even the bathroom walls. As I grew up, I still loved playing with makeup and my parents encouraged me to go for it.

One winter, while home from college, I told my mother that I wanted to drop out of school. She said I couldn't and insisted that I get a college degree – and I thank her for it. She asked me what I wanted to do when I finished school and I had no idea. Then she said something that is so simple, but changed my life. She said, 'Forget about what you want to do with your life – pretend it's your birthday and you can do anything you want.' I stopped and said I wanted to go to Marshall Fields (a Chicago department store) and play with makeup. And she said, 'Why don't you study cosmetics and get a degree from a school somewhere?' My passion for makeup led me to Emerson College in Boston where I pursued a degree in theatrical makeup.

After graduating from college with a degree in theatrical makeup design, I headed to New York to fulfill my dream of working as a professional makeup artist. It was the 1980s and the look of the moment was loud, garish and overdone. I soon became frustrated by the lack of flattering makeup on the market. It was impossible to find makeup that looked good on the skin. I almost always had to mix the products I bought, blending shades together until I got something that looked natural. I saw a major void in the cosmetics industry that I knew I could help address. My vision was to create a cosmetics line that looked natural and would match and complement women's complexions. I started with creating lipstick shades that made lips look like lips, only better.

I had an idea to develop a flattering lipstick – something that was different from everything available in stores. I realised that not everybody loved neutrals, so I thought about ten different women I knew and what colours would look good on them. With this set of ten lipsticks, a woman could create an infinite number of wearable shades, just by mixing and blending them. After launching my original ten lipsticks at Bergdorf Goodman in February 1991, I knew a beauty revolution was underway. Women really embraced these uniquely flattering shades and my realistic approach to beauty.

The launch of Bobbi Brown at Bergdorf Goodman in 1991 was an iconic moment for me and I remember it like it was yesterday. I thought we would sell 100 lipsticks in the first month, and we sold 100 in the first day.

# Bobbi's
# *ADVICE*

- You need a unique idea, you need to be passionate about your craft and you have to work hard.

- Don't stop at the first hurdle that you meet. You must keep your goal in mind and move forward.

- And most importantly, you need to trust your instincts.

Credit: Tomas De A Fuente

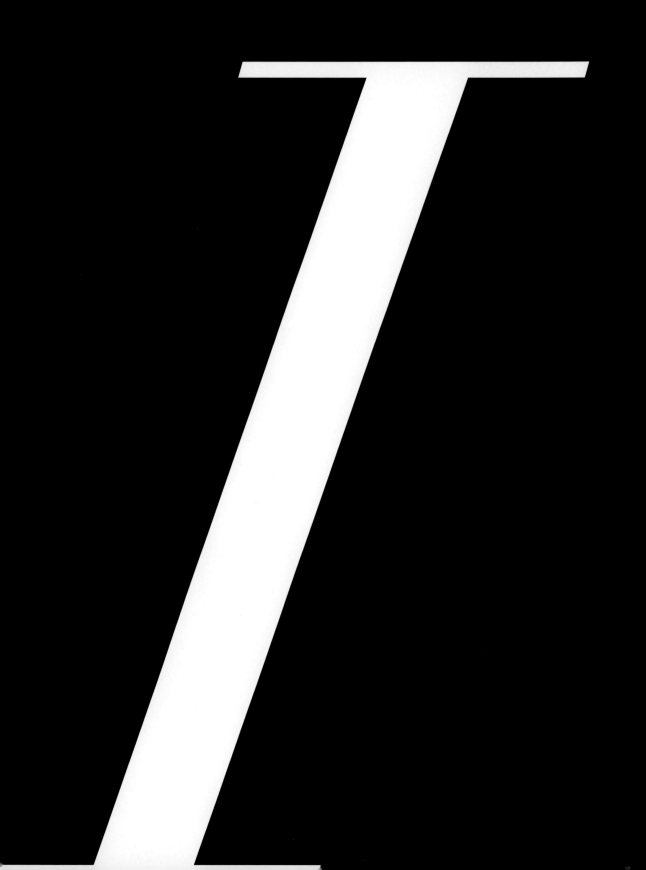

*IN ORDER
TO BE
IRREPLACEABLE,
ONE MUST
ALWAYS BE
DIFFERENT*

COCO CHANEL

# MOTTO

*Enjoy the journey as much as the destination.*

# MEGAN HESS

FASHION ILLUSTRATOR

*Megan Hess is an international fashion illustrator and has been called
upon by some of the most prestigious fashion designers and luxury brands
around the world, including Chanel, Prada, Dior and Louis Vuitton. In 2008,
she illustrated the bestselling* Sex and the City *book by Candace Bushnell.
Her works can now be seen at leading hotels, in numerous books and on
the walls of global fashion houses. She is the creative patron for the
Ovarian Cancer Research Foundation.*

I studied Graphic Design because it felt like a 'real' job in the art world, but I really always wanted to be an illustrator – I just never knew back then that it was a possible career choice! After working as an art director in advertising agencies for several years, I packed everything up and moved from Australia to London. It was in London that I worked in a million different creative jobs and in my final job there, I realised that I had a burning desire to be an artist.

At this time, I became the art director for Liberty department store. While I loved art directing fashion, I loved illustrating it more. I started to do very small illustrations for Liberty and from this, art directors saw my work and little commissions began to follow. After about a year I found myself with nonstop work. I wasn't earning a fortune, but I'd never been happier and I knew I was going to do this forever.

As my clients got bigger and better, I was able to be a little more selective and just work on briefs that I knew had a great creative opportunity. Then in 2006, I got a call in the middle of the night from Candace Bushnell's publisher, asking if I would illustrate her next novel, *One Fifth Avenue*. This was when things took off at rapid speed for me. Her book became a *New York Times* bestseller. I later met with Candace and she asked me to illustrate all her previous books including the cover of *Sex and the City*. Once *Sex and the City* was released, I was contacted by *TIME* magazine in New York to create portraits for them. This was a dream come true and I still can't believe I work for them. Following this, I began illustrating for Tiffany & Co, Chanel, Dior, Cartier, *Vanity Fair*, Italian *Vogue*, Bergdorf Goodman, Prada, Salvatore Ferragamo ... Ironically, at the same time as my work finally took off, I had my first baby! It's funny, I always tell people that I haven't really slept since 2006!

## THE CHALLENGES

The biggest challenge has been managing it all! In the very beginning, the struggle was to find great projects to work on. I initially had no clients and I wasn't yet a mother, so the challenge was to get things moving. Then once my work took on after *Sex and The City* I had the opposite problem – I had lots of great projects and brands coming to me to collaborate so it was quite overwhelming.

Today, I still find the biggest challenge juggling it all. I can now only take on about 20 per cent of the jobs that come to me each year, so I have to be very careful about what projects are the best – I've learned that it's better to do a smaller number of jobs at 100 per cent then lots of jobs at 50 per cent. At the end of the day, I try to base this decision on what projects will have the best creative outcome – some projects have huge budgets and others are tiny, but I always choose to work on projects that will fulfill me creatively.

I've always believed that ability will only get you so far and attitude, however, is everything. I think that in the very beginning (before *Sex and the City*), I gave 100 per cent to every single illustration job that came my way. Most of the projects that came to me in the very beginning were *not* inspiring. For example, I was asked to illustrate a 300-page horse manual that on completion was cancelled! After six months of work, I received a tiny 'kill fee' and really felt like giving up on my dream of becoming a fashion illustrator. Another soul destroying job that almost made me give up was a pizza toppings illustration for a pizza company. I remember very clearly the day I finished drawing that – I turned off the light in my studio at the end of the day and thought to myself 'I think its time to give up'. That very night at 3 a.m. was when I received the call from Candace Bushnell's publisher and my life changed forever. In short, I think never giving up is the biggest lesson I've learned.

I feel my biggest achievement is getting paid to do what I love for a living and being a mother. I see it as a huge luxury to be able to do both and it's something that I'm very grateful for every day. I've also been able to donate many pieces of my work for charities and causes all over the world and I feel proud that, in some small way, one of my drawings may have helped someone somewhere. As Creative Patron of Ovarian Cancer Research Foundation, I've also had the privilege of working with the most inspiring team of people trying into raise awareness and funds for the development of an early detection test for ovarian cancer.

## INSPIRATIONS

My parents were always very supportive of my dreams and always made me feel like anything was possible. In high school, I had an amazing art teacher who helped me build a sense of confidence to pursue drawing. Later in life, I have really been inspired by so many other creative people all over the world who I have worked with. I learned to take advice, to really listen and see what makes other people interesting or creative. Even people who are difficult or demanding to work with, there is still always knowledge to be gained by the experience of working together. Above all, I have learned that no matter what anyone else feels, you have to go with your gut.

One of my favourite collaborations has been with Tiffany & Co in New York.

# Megan's TIPS

- Decide what is the one thing that would make you excited to spring out of bed on a Monday morning and do for a career.

- Write down a plan and strategy to make that dream happen and start on it *today*.

- You don't need to suddenly quit your current job or dramatically change your life but taking the first step is always the hardest.

- Never, ever give up on that dream. If it's something that you love, then you will enjoy the process, regardless of the outcome.

I was asked to illustrate their iconic 5th Avenue building filled with chic Tiffany & Co people in the foreground! It was a dream project. Another collaboration that was wonderful to work on was with Cartier in Paris. It all centred around Paris Fashion Week and I created ten bespoke illustrations for their Paris Nouvelle Vague collection. Recently I collaborated with Prada in Milan on an animation for their Autumn Winter Collection – the creative process of that job was probably one of the most exciting. In terms of individuals, I have worked on some very exciting (and nerve-racking) portraits – everyone from Gwyneth Paltrow, Jennifer Lopez to Michelle Obama.

## GLOBAL REACH

Working globally continues to be a challenge. Today, it's probably one of the things that I love most about what I do because it's incredibly exciting to work with different brands and projects all over the world. The problem initially was that all my work was coming from New York and Europe and communicating and travelling with a newborn baby was very hard! Even if I wasn't travelling, I was always Skyping late at night and early in the morning and then illustrating all day long – it was very hard to have any time to switch off. Now, I have my communicating with overseas clients down to a fine art. For all my US clients, I wake at 6 a.m. – I do my makeup and hair in six minutes – I keep my PJ's on the bottom half and I wear something chic on the top half (because that's all they can see on Skype), then I do the Skype before my kids are even awake. Then I'm off to my day. I'll do a late night Skype the next night to Europe – but never the two on the same day. I also condense my travelling to what is really necessary. Everything is planning. If I can really hone the schedule of any work trip, it becomes both productive and enjoyable.

     I did find the juggling of all the projects that I work on very overwhelming at times. Even though I was working on many dream projects, the stress of getting it all done could outweigh the joy that I should have felt. The greatest thing that I did to combat that stress was learn to meditate. In the beginning, it was so hard to quieten the mind – it felt impossible. But I didn't give up on it and once it clicked and began working, it changed my life. Initially, I could only do ten minutes but now I can easily do twenty minutes of meditation and it feels like I've completely recharged my battery. It's really made me feel like I can tackle any issue without stress and to me that's a very powerful thing.

*THE WOMEN WHO I LOVE AND ADMIRE FOR THEIR STRENGTH AND GRACE DID NOT GET THAT WAY BECAUSE IT WORKED OUT. THEY GOT THAT WAY BECAUSE THINGS WENT WRONG AND THEY HANDLED IT. THOSE WOMEN ARE MY SUPERHEROES*

**ELIZABETH GILBERT**

# MOTTO

*'Happiness is a choice, not a result. Your happiness will not come to you. It can only come from you.'* *This quote makes me feel so empowered and inspired, and I hope it makes others feel the same and realise they can take control of their own life like I did.*

# ELLA MILLS

BESTSELLING AUTHOR, HEALTH ENTREPENEUR

*Ella Mills is an award-winning author. She writes the popular website Deliciously Ella, and is a champion of eating well. Her first book has been the bestselling debut cookbook ever in the UK, an Amazon bestseller, a New York Times bestseller and has been translated into fifteen languages. She's since written three more bestsellers.*

Before I became ill, back in 2011, I was studying History of Art at St Andrews University. I was a normal student and was looking to work within the art world. In June that year, I suddenly got ill and that changed everything. After months in hospital having test after test, I was diagnosed with Postural Tachycardia Syndrome, a chronic illness that affects the autonomic nervous system, stopping it from working as it should – so I couldn't regulate my heart rate, circulation, digestions and immune system, amongst other issues. I tried conventional medicine for about six months but sadly this didn't help as much as I had hoped and I was still bedridden most of the time. That's when I decided to look at diet and lifestyle as tools for managing the symptoms and looked towards a natural, plant-based approach. It took me about eighteen months to start getting my symptoms under control and come off my medication and a further year or two on top of that to feel pretty normal.

**THE CHALLENGES**

Overcoming my illness was so hard for me, both mentally and physically. As well as the everyday physical challenges, I really struggled with depression and isolation. I struggled to keep going and push forward at this time and although the end results were positive, it absolutely wasn't uphill all the way – I'd have so many bad days when I was fighting so hard for good ones, which was a real challenge. Likewise, I made progress in some areas but others took a long time to see any change and I still have to be careful to manage the condition, which can be hard as it does still mean daily limitations, but I can really live my life now.

**CREATING DELICIOUSLY ELLA**

I'm so lucky that Deliciously Ella happened very organically. I started the blog as a way of teaching myself how to cook and to document what I was learning. It's come a long way since then. I've now written four books, launched a bestselling app, opened two delis in London and launched a product line into stores across the UK.

I think when it comes to creating a brand around yourself, being authentic is the most important aspect. You have to embrace who you are and share that. People see straight through fake personalities – especially in the world of social media. I think it is just sheer determination, confidence in what you're doing and a real passion for what you do. It's important to develop a tough skin too; criticism is really important for growth, so we all need to learn to embrace negative comments and learn from them and, at the same time, learn when to tune it out.

As we've grown into more areas it's been so important to stay true to the core values of Deliciously Ella; this is something that we work on everyday to ensure that they're consistent across all our projects.

I couldn't have built what I have without the people around me though, finding a strong team is everything. I really believe a business is only as good as the people in it, and I've learned so much from everyone I'm lucky enough to work with.

# *Ella's* ADVICE

- Be genuine, authentic and yourself. Find your voice and be consistent with it, and always engage with your audience.

- Drop your ego and surround yourself with fantastic people who can help you drive your vision forward. Learn from them, listen to the criticism and don't be afraid to admit when you're wrong.

- Never give up and always be an optimist. Everyone wants to quit sometimes, but the people who succeed are the ones who keep pushing through. See the daily challenges as learning curves that make you better, so that you keep growing.

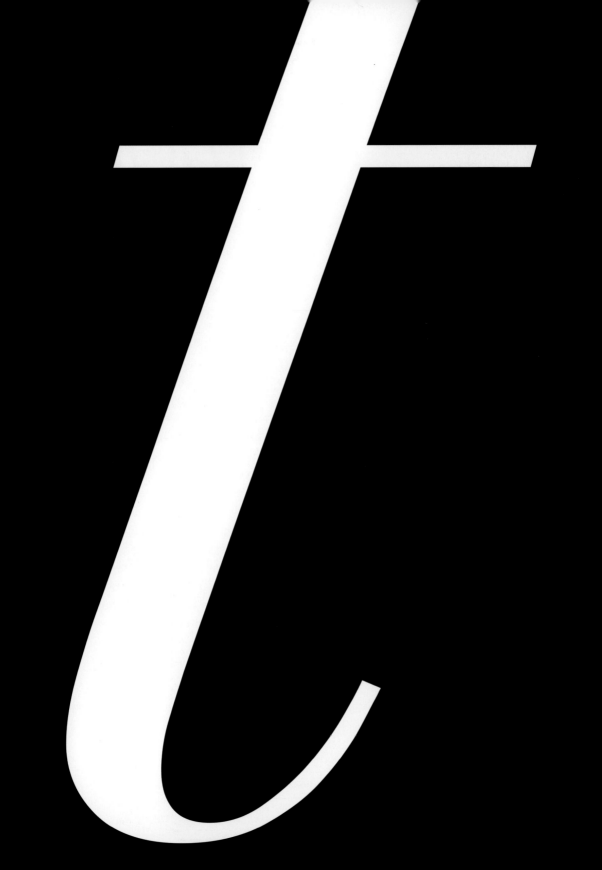

# THERE ARE SECRET OPPORTUNITIES HIDDEN IN EVERY FAILURE

SOPHIA AMORUSO

MOTTO

*Impossible is nothing.*

# LANA HOPKINS

### FOUNDER AND CEO OF MON PURSE

*As the creator of monogrammed leather goods brand Mon Purse,*
*Lana Hopkins has proven dreams really can come true with hard work*
*and persistence. The brand is now a worldwide phenomenon and coveted*
*by celebrities around the globe.*

The ability to make a real difference in the world has always been the driving force behind my ambition. Upon completing high school I studied International Business and Marketing at the University of Technology Sydney (I now sit on the board of my alma mater, an institution I greatly admire for its progressive approach to education, especially technology).

I came from a media background and I worked in magazine advertising sales at News Ltd. I was also part of another start-up, founded by my very talented husband James, as Marketing and Sales Director prior to founding Mon Purse. This invaluable experience paved the way for Mon Purse.

## THE INSPIRATION

I saw a gap in the luxury leather bag market. I realised that I simply spent far too many hours pounding the pavement, looking for the perfect handbag. I wanted to solve this personal problem – the ability to have the perfect handbag, with the leather, hardware, lining and size that I wanted, to suit my personal style. I wanted it to smell, feel and look premium and luxurious (made in Europe) without the astronomical price tag. And I wanted the unforgettable experience of actually designing my perfect bag online, much like I had felt when I created my very own Teddy Bear (at the Teddy Bear Factory) at Westfield, Bondi Junction as a gift. If it was possible for kids to build their own teddy bears, people to create their own custom Nike shoes, and fashionable women around the world to design their own premium women's shoes, there simply had to be a way to create high quality, luxury and bespoke handbags.

I had a vision to create an elegant, state of the art bag builder, and then follow this up with high quality, customisable and bespoke creations, delivered to your door. So, during 2014, I travelled the world looking for the best tanneries and ateliers, hand selected quality leathers and raw materials, and employed incredibly skilled craftsmen. I also found some great software engineers to turn our vision into reality.

I still have to pinch myself that we only launched online in October 2014. Which means that we've really been trading for less than a year and a half now, but in that time so much has changed. We have opened the doors to our Paddington flagship and signed an exclusive deal with Myer, for example. We have collaborated with incredibly inspiring women like Laura Brown and most recently partnered with two of the most prestigious department stores in the world. Remembering how far we have come in such a short period of time is a source of constant pride for me.

**OVERSEAS EXPANSION**

In 2016, my co-founder Andrew Shub and I went to the UK hoping to meet with Selfridges. Likewise, we visited New York in August to meet with Bloomingdale's. We got a yes from Selfridges and Bloomingdale's the day we pitched, which is fairly unheard of. The teams at both Selfridges and Bloomingdale's were incredibly blown away by the Mon Purse bag builder technology and product quality and execution. They told us that had never seen anything like it before.

Our assumption initially was that it would take in excess of twelve months for a potential deal to materialise, which is the industry norm. Furthermore to be offered the first Australian full line concession deal was beyond our wildest expectations. We are incredibly proud to represent Australian style and innovation in the Northern Hemisphere. Selfridges and Bloomingdale's are globally recognised retail pioneers so the alignment with both in time for Christmas 2016 was an absolute honour for Mon Purse. In all honesty, this is a true 'pinch me' moment, as we launched in beta (online) two years ago and have only been truly trading for less than one and a half years.

During this time we managed to open our Paddington flagship store, signed an exclusive deal with Myer (we currently have five concessions Australia wide, with more to come over the next few years). So a partnership with two of the most prestigious department

stores in the world is humbling and incredibly inspirational for our team.

This win validates my personal core belief, shared by the rest of the business, that impossible is nothing. If you wish to be to be a global brand negotiating and opening doors into these markets you need to be bold and demonstrate that you are insanely passionate and above all can deliver.

## THE MON PURSE MOTTO

At Mon Purse, we believe in being fearless, passionate and strategic. Andrew and I sat together and started to brainstorm how we would possibly break into the global markets. We both knew we had a truly unique concept, a world first in this space, but the real question was how to communicate this to real decision makers. We both have very complementary skills and our ability to focus and utilise these skills from different perspectives I believe was the ultimate 'door opener'.

We strongly believe in playing to your strengths and your team's strengths and anything is achievable. Behind the scenes we used our collaborative skill set first to build a world class proposition. We had already proved that we could execute in the Australian marketplace and we used this as a case study to create and build an out of the box presentation. Use the skills available to you, prepare beyond belief, be fearless, proactive and use your network – they will surprise you. For Andrew, myself and the team this is a dream come true and we wouldn't change one thing about it.

## THE CHALLENGES

The biggest challenge with global expansion is having to be in more than one place at the one time. We feel aligning the brand with ambassadors who celebrate the ethos of the brand's offering contributes to its success. Meaningful collaboration is fundamental to the brand strategy, like partnering with Jodi Anasta, Australian model and actress, who designed a capsule range for Mon Purse, in addition to having digital influencer and stylemaker Margaret Zhang on board earlier in 2016 as Creative Director to cultivate an overarching aesthetic and execute creative concepts. Also, cementing Mon Purse's position as an innovative brand through meaningful partnerships such as with Laura Brown, fellow Australian and Editor in Chief of *Instyle* US, who recently launched the newest range in New York.

We've gone from 17 million design combinations to 6 billion and growing on our 3D bag builder. I've definitely learned that nothing can be achieved without the support of an incredible team. My incredible team as well as my supportive husband, Andrew, have been my inspirations and advisors along the way. I've also had business advisors and mentors, and, of course, my family helping me along the way. We have recently joined forces with superwoman Laura Brown, funny, witty and one of a kind. Laura was incredibly hands-on and passionate about every aspect of the design process and her energy is absolutely contagious.

Of course we have many challenges – online retailers are everywhere and often as you solve one challenge you create another two or three that you never knew you had. The solutions are driven by smart new technologies that address and over-come problems. In the next five years, I see myself creating opportunities for women and young entrepreneurs, supporting and mentoring them through their journeys to successful careers.

# Lana's TIPS

- Focus on one thing at a time and always back yourself.

- When it gets too hard, just keep going because that is when breakthroughs tend to happen.

- Nothing can be achieved without the support of an incredible team.

- Just do it, because nothing is impossible.

- Never forget why you started on this incredible journey (for me it was all about making women insanely happy with an amazing product they could get truly excited about) and keep the passion alive.

# MOTTO

*Where the mind goes, the energy flows. From a business perspective, we work to the idea of 'suck it and see'. Try something small and see how it goes and then build on the idea or the direction as it feels right, getting real-time feedback from the zeitgeist around you.*

# SARAH WILSON

CREATOR OF I QUIT SUGAR, *NEW YORK TIMES* BESTSELLING
AUTHOR

*Sarah Wilson is an Australian journalist, TV presenter and former editor of*
*Cosmopolitan magazine. When she embarked on her journey to quit sugar*
*and improve her health, she knew women the world over would benefit from*
*everything she had learned, so she compiled her knowledge into a series of*
*ebooks and programs, which have now helped more than 1.2 million people*
*quit sugar. Sarah is now the go-to girl for health inspiration.*

I was a journalist for years and then I found myself living in an army shed in the forest in the Byron Bay hinterland, trying to work out what to do with my life. A mid-thirties crisis. I was recovering from a severe illness and was merely focused on getting better. Quitting sugar was part of that. Social media was starting to take off and so I developed a community based around my journey. I'd developed a conversation online and the community was part of the process the whole way, so they became my mouthpieces. My message is particularly 'organic' and my style is not to be didactic.

It was at this point that I went down the rabbit hole, seeking answers and better science. The first ebook that emerged from that was titled *I Quit Sugar*. I was then asked to turn *I Quit Sugar* into a program, which I did. I learned how to make ebooks and about six months later, print publishers approached me about turning it into a print book. It all unfurled by happenstance. Which is exactly how I run my business now – trusting that things will unfurl as they need to. I respond as life posits a challenge in front of me!

A big part of the 8-Week Program and my business as a whole is the notion of working to the idea that what I present should be a gentle invitation and a gentle experiment. I think this is what resonated in an era of aggressive, bossy, diet plans (that don't work).

## EXPANDING THE BRAND

The biggest challenge was ensuring that I maintained my health and values while obviously having to push quite hard to keep up with where the business was heading. I also had to make the call to move back to Sydney to continue the work. I had to find a way to make this not feel like a compromise, but rather, another gentle experiment.

Through my I Quit Sugar business online, we now have twelve ebooks available, and two of those are available in print as well (we self-published).

I also have three I Quit Sugar print books I've released (with my publisher), to continue to respond to the needs of those around the world who are quitting sugar. It's an elegant business model and when you work online, you have real time interactions that can guide the ship.

I feel like the luckiest girl on the planet to have a career that actually allows me to do what I told my mother I wanted to do from the age of five or six – to make the world better (at seven, I told mum I'd be the first female Prime Minister of Australia; I think I landed in a better gig). I was fortunate enough to take a myopic, obsessed interest in the science of sugar as it was emerging. It was the right timing. But I think the fact the message is not pushy enabled people to come to the idea when it suited them, which is vital when you're talking about making a big change in your life.

# Sarah's
# *ADVICE*

- Create something first and then trust that the community/customers will follow, when it's the right time.

- Believe in what you're doing. If you don't have a solid belief in what you're creating, the world will 'smell' the lack of authenticity and wobbliness in your own intention. But once you hit that spot where you truly believe in what you're doing, steer your energy fully and convincingly in that direction.

*WHEN THE WHOLE WORLD IS SILENT, EVEN ONE VOICE BECOMES POWERFUL*

**MALALA YOUSAFZAI**

# MOTTO

*'Always remember your focus
determines your reality.'*

*– George Lucas.
It's not so much inspirational as
it is reality. You see direct results
from focus.*

# ALMIRA ARMSTRONG

## FOUNDER OF LUMIRA

*Almira Armstrong is the founder of Lumira candles. After starting out her career as an internet entrepreneur, she saw a gap in the market for afford-able, quality, beautiful candles – and is now providing exclusive ranges to some of the top hotels in the world.*

Prior to starting Lumira, I was always involved with building other brands – whether it be from a PR, marketing or sales perspective. I worked for a time with Marcs and Diesel, as well as a hotel group.

An old friend and I started an online business that offered templated website solutions – we would design clean, beautiful templates for budding start-ups and creatives who didn't necessarily have the budget to invest, at least initially, in designers and developers. I was in my twenties and knew of many people who had little to no budget, but really didn't want to compromise on beautiful design for their websites.

We had an opportunity to introduce the product to clients in the US and Los Angeles, being the tech savvy city that it is, was incredibly welcoming. The business very much grew within the creative industries in LA – photographers, filmmakers and the like were very engaged with what we were doing and it did really well for that reason. My friend and I are both quite tech savvy and certainly put the time into learning, appreciating and honing our skillset when it came to design and digital practice. However, we still had to learn all that goes with creating your own start-up – particularly one that intends to support the work of other start-ups – and that, in itself, was quite challenging. Our greatest success was getting the business off the ground, watching it flourish and seeing other brands succeed because of a solution we had put in place. I think, for us, having the opportunity to take the product overseas and introduce it to the American market was a huge 'pinch me' moment.

Deciding to leave the business didn't rest on one concrete moment. It was very much about timing. An opportunity arose for me to further my career and I couldn't turn it down. I moved across to Sun Studios and it was honestly one of the best working experiences I had, acting in the role of General Manager and Marketing Manager.

## THE BIRTH OF LUMIRA

When my husband and I moved back to Australia from the United States, my son was a newborn (and my first child), so that was my next exciting challenge. I always knew I wanted to go back to work, but balancing a new role with a baby – that was going to be quite tricky. I happened to be telling my husband about how I used to develop scents and candles for friends while I was at university as a hobby. It was so nice to create something special for them. He said my eyes just lit up when I spoke about it. I remember him saying, 'This is what you need to do!' He had ideas about me holding market stalls. I knew I wanted to take it further than that and now it's three years later and Lumira is still going!

The biggest challenge for me was right at the beginning of starting Lumira. Deciding how big or small you want your business to go, in many ways, needs to be considered from the beginning. This is particularly the case when you are looking at budget projections, how you are going to incorporate stockists, a team – there isn't one part of the business that should be overlooked.

The inspiration for Lumira comes from far and wide. At the time (and still to this day), it didn't come directly from seeing another brand or scent that I really loved. In fact, it was more directly related to travel. Travel plays a huge part in how I develop my product. I was motivated by asking myself; 'How can I be so inspired by the places I have been to and translate those memories into a product?'

Thematically, each fragrance I develop – whether it be for a candle or a wearable fragrance – is derivative of a time and place that has struck a chord with me. Communicating this to my husband and to close friends, whose opinion I trust, motivated me to take that next step and launch the business.

THE LITTLE BLACK JACKET    CARINE ROITFELD

PETER LINDBERGH
THE LITTLE BLACK JACKET
CARINE ROITFELD
LUMIRA.
CUBAN TOBACCO
Tobacco, Patchouli
& Cardamom
SCENTED CANDLE

## THE CHALLENGES

My biggest challenge has come both personally and professionally. From a personal level, I've really learned to let go. I can't do everything, I just don't have the time. And I have a team that I really trust. However, when you have built a business from scratch, learning to let go can be quite confronting. From a business level, the biggest challenge is learning all those things that it takes to run a successful business – even the more arduous admin components. While it would be dreamy to just create scents or work on product development each and every day, it just isn't viable for building a well-rounded business.

I think focusing on my own path and my own brand has really ensured Lumira stayed on the right track over the last three years. I think comparing yourself to other brands that play within the same space can be hugely detrimental to the success of what you are creating. That's not to say you should be naïve about how the market is growing and shifting, but really knowing what your business goals and objectives are – that's so much more important. From a creative point of view, each and every product I create is developed from scratch. I don't select scents off the shelf. I'm also quite particular (a true Virgo) about quality control. I check over everything – the wax, the glass vessel, the wick, the box – before it goes out to a customer, store or media!

If you had asked me two years ago what was my biggest achievement, I would have said making it through the first year with Lumira. I think it's a good indicator of business longevity if you can make it through year one. It's fun and exciting, but incredibly hard work too. I think for me, one of the biggest achievements has been securing incredible, reputable stockists. I wouldn't exist without their support. Every day there are little achievements that need to be celebrated. They all end up as part of the bigger picture!

## GROWING THE BRAND

First and foremost, my husband has been someone who has supported me throughout this venture. I'm very grateful for his support. Not only as a husband and father in our little family unit, but also for his savvy business mind. He has certainly imparted some wisdom when it comes to making big decisions. We built the brand together and while he has stepped away from the day-to-day now, I feel really inspired by his business acumen and just having that other person to brainstorm with and run ideas by. I'm also incredibly inspired by the many people who I have crossed paths with – whether it be collaborators, journalists or stockists.

They each have their own path and story to tell, which is always fascinating and inspiring in and of itself.

Up to this point, I have focused heavily on PR, digital and social media to promote Lumira. These are such strong channels to get a small business out into the market. With planning and strategy, you can really determine who it is that you want to target and how you want them to receive the brand. When you are working with smaller budgets – or when I started in 2013 with no budget at all – you need channels of exposure that are willing to tell your story authentically and in an engaging manner, without jeopardising what you stand for. I would say this has definitely been a huge driver of the success of the brand. From the outset I wanted to create a luxury product that didn't compromise on quality or aesthetics. While sometimes it has cost me more than other routes I could have taken, I would never change the way our product is made or designed. Having an Australian product, I think, is a huge key to our success.

Our Emirates One&Only Wolgan Valley candle was such an exciting collaboration – one that was in the works for close to a year. It was quite a natural alignment, as Lumira is already available with the resort spa. However, when we decided to work together on the bespoke candle, I visited the resort and met the team who was driving the project from their end. We discussed scent inspirations and the overall feel they wanted to create when the candle was lit. Unsurprisingly, the candle has been a great success. I think the passion of both brands shines through in the final product.

**THE SETBACKS**

There have been plenty of setbacks of course, and I learn from them, work through them and get back on track. When you are working with consumer goods, you are working with lots of suppliers, materials and levels of expertise. There are always going to be moments when something might come back not exactly the way you envisioned it. However, you learn from it, continue working toward best practice and move forward!

While it sounds obvious and aspiring entrepreneurs reading this may think, 'I need something more concrete advice-wise', I can't express it enough that my best piece of advice would be to just give it a go. Really just put your heart and soul into it. Don't be (too) dlsheartened if you come up against challenges and setbacks – we all do. We just don't necessarily broadcast it.

**THE FUTURE**

In the next few years, I see myself continuing to build and nurture the Lumira brand. I would love for the brand to be in a place where I can grow the team. In saying that, I do love working with a small team. I also have big visions around how I would like to extend our offering and really tap into different areas that translate the essence of a design and travel-led lifestyle!

# *Almira's top* 5 TIPS

- Clichéd as it sounds, stay true to your vision and focus on it!

- Create a business plan and run it past someone you trust and, preferably, who has knowledge. Understand your budget, your business trajectory and the market you are playing in.

- Don't underestimate the power of collaboration. You are not the master of all things – surround yourself with experts and let them do their thing. You will reap the rewards and they will as well.

- Make sure to educate yourself, to some degree, in all areas of your business. Know what can directly or indirectly impact your business – both negative and positive forces!

- Find time to just do you. Get a massage, treat yourself to a nice lunch, read a book – do something (anything!) that helps you unwind. You will burn out otherwise and it's so important to look after yourself in the early days of your business as you will constantly be putting in 110 per cent and it's easy to burn out.

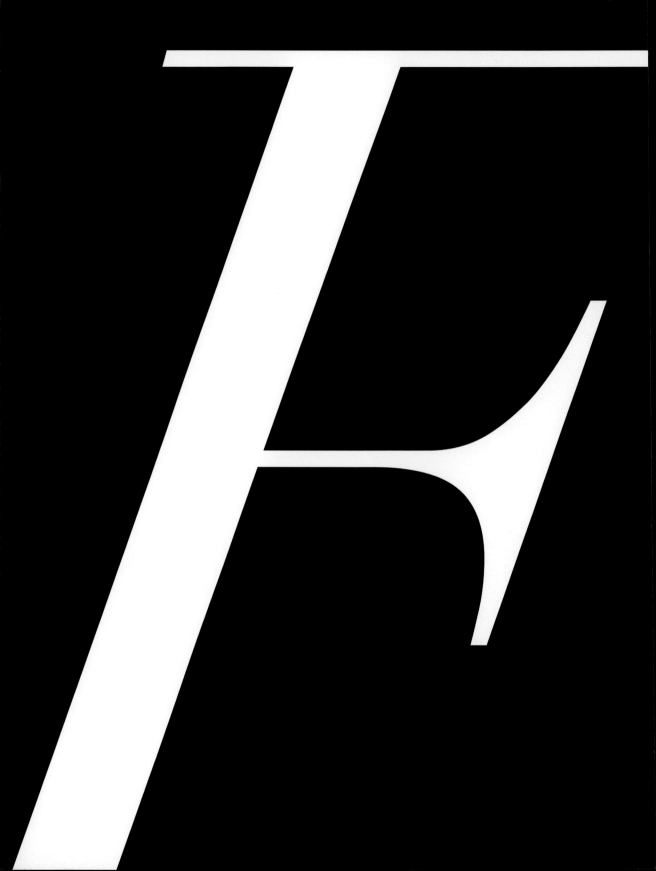

*FIND OUT WHO YOU ARE AND BE THAT PERSON. THAT'S WHAT YOUR SOUL WAS PUT ON THIS EARTH TO BE. FIND THAT TRUTH, LIVE THAT TRUTH AND EVERYTHING ELSE WILL COME*

**ELLEN DEGENERES**

# MOTTO

*Control the controllable. And occasionally I remind myself that 'shit happens'!*

# MELISSA DOYLE

## AWARD-WINNING TELEVISION NEWS HOST, JOURNALIST, AUTHOR

*Melissa Doyle is an Australian television favourite with a hugely successful career spanning more than twenty-five years, from hosting Australia's number one breakfast show for more than a decade, to the 6 p.m. news and now the host and senior correspondent of Seven's flagship news and a current affairs program* Sunday Night. *She is a multi-award-winning journalist and has covered many notable news events both in Australia and around the world, including hours of uninterrupted live coverage during the Martin Place Siege in 2014. She is a bestselling author and spokesperson for a number of charities.*

I'd wanted to be a journalist since I was about twelve. Every school holidays I'd go anywhere I could to get any sort of work experience: *The Manly Daily*, the graveyard shift at 2GB, a television station in Coffs Harbour. And if they said they didn't take work experience kids, I convinced them to let me come in as the tea maker or newspaper sorter. Anything to get in the door of a newsroom!

I studied Communications at Charles Stuart University in Bathurst and had my heart set on TV journalism. I got a job as a cadet reporter at WIN TV in Canberra about a month before finishing uni so luckily they let me use on-air reports as practical work so I could graduate. I filed an average of two stories a day and I was the weather girl for our nightly 6 p.m. bulletin.

## THE EARLY CHALLENGES

I honestly don't remember the early challenges! Maybe I've blotted it out. I remember working hard, taking every opportunity, giving anything a go. I do remember being frustrated when I couldn't always get the breaks I wanted. The weather position became available not long after I started at WIN, and I remember finally convincing the boss to give me a go in the role one Friday night. I said if I was terrible I'd never bug him about it again. I don't think I was very good, but I did get the job. I had the same attitude when I knocked on the door at Seven News. I offered to work for free just to be given the opportunity to prove myself.

Career breaks can be the combination of a few things – right place at the right time – but you've got to be good enough to walk through the door when it opens in front of you and have worked hard enough to actually get there. And sometimes you have got to back yourself. I think it takes a few years to work out your strengths and weaknesses. And I think both are equally important to recognise and embrace.

## HOSTING A BREAKFAST SHOW

It was an incredible opportunity to work on *Sunrise*. We were able to build a show from the ground up into what it is today. I remember celebrating when we got to 50 000 viewers. Because we started under the radar, we were able to find our own way, totally by ourselves, stand up for issues we believed in, give the program soul and heart, and let it grow naturally. Viewers started to come along with us for the ride and we really created a *Sunrise* family. We could try a new way of doing things – we became 'Mel and Kochie' instead of the more formal Melissa Doyle and David Koch (my co-host). We read viewer emails on air and campaigned for issues that hadn't traditionally been getting attention in that sort of format. I am very proud of what we achieved. I'd be lying if I didn't admit it was tough though. Getting up at 3 a.m. for fourteen years. Having two babies during that time. Sleep and nightly TV were two things I missed for a very long time.

## STORY HIGHLIGHTS

I can't name one. I love the mix that my job brings. I remember standing outside Kerobokan jail in the middle of a media scrum in stifling heat waiting for Schapelle Corby's release and two weeks later wearing a long gown on the Oscars red carpet chatting to Hugh Jackman. That contrast makes it interesting and I think it makes me a better journalist.

Of course it is always fun to interview the big names and it's given me some great dinner party stories! Tom Cruise the day after Suri was born, Robin Williams, Katy Perry, Justin Bieber, Jane Fonda. But it's also been the people I have met in other circumstances that have affected me the most: survivors of the Black Saturday bushfires and the Queensland floods, the Beaconsfield miners.

The part of my job I treasure the most is having the opportunity to stand somewhere at a moment in history as a representative of our viewers – the papal election in Rome, President Obama's inauguration, the centenary of Gallipoli – it's my job to tell you what it feels like, sounds like, smells like, why it is significant and matters. It is a privilege I will never take for granted.

## FROM BREAKFAST TO NIGHTLY NEWS

It didn't take long to adjust to sleeping past 3 a.m. The first few weeks after I switched from morning to nightly news, I had lunches made, breakfast ready, two loads of washing done and the kitchen tidy by 5.30 a.m.! The best part was having my nights back. My hubby had the remote and the couch to himself for so long; suddenly I was able to enjoy a glass of wine with him and watch TV or, even better, go out for dinner midweek! I was able to enjoy the next step in my career.

## THE MARTIN PLACE SIEGE

I am honestly grateful that in my twenty-five years of experience as a journalist and of live TV I got to cover the story of the Lindt Café siege over those few days. I felt such an overwhelming sense of responsibility. I was mindful of every word I spoke, imagining that the hostages' families might be watching and not wanting to make them any more frightened than they would already be; that the gunman might have a television on in the café and

I didn't want to say or show anything that could jeopardise the police operation; and people including children were watching, probably terrified about what could happen. It wasn't the time to create unnecessary alarm or sensationalise the events of the day in any way. I think the mum in me kicked in and I knew I had to relay what was happening but in a way that didn't create unnecessary fear. At one stage I abruptly ended an interview when the guest started talking about the modus operandi of Al-Qaeda and their propensity for beheadings. I didn't think that was the time or place.

There is certainly an element of adrenalin that rushes through you when you are working under those circumstances. I was standing on Elizabeth Street, on the edge of the police cordon, with nothing but a camera in front of me. Because our newsroom had been evacuated, we were broadcasting via the control room in Melbourne and at one point from Perth. The entire team did an exceptional job to get us to air over those few days. But that is our job, and no matter how tired we got, I knew it would be worse inside the café .

## THE GLASS CEILING

I'd like to think viewers recognise credibility and accept someone who can do their job well – male or female. Although a woman tends to attract a little more criticism about her appearance than a man does, unfortunately.

## BEING APPOINTED MEMBER OF THE ORDER OF AUSTRALIA

I have been given a voice and a profile and I feel very strongly about making the most of this unique opportunity. Some people are rich enough to build a wing on a hospital, some smart enough to cure cancer. I have a voice I chose to use. I am a patron and an ambassador for a number of charities and they have opened my eyes to sick children, struggling families. I'm really grateful I have had the chance to do something to help. My travels with World Vision have shaped me as a person. Even our poorest have access to electricity, clean drinking water, sanitation, free education and health care.

## BIGGEST ACHIEVEMENT

Raising two gorgeous, kind, sweet children. It's never easy for any parent. There have been times as a working mum that I've found it particularly challenging and wondered if I was stretching myself bit too thin. But so far so good! And in terms of my profession, I'd like to think I'm open minded, balanced and fair.

## THE BIGGEST CHALLENGE

Probably simply overcoming my own self doubts. Wondering if I'm good enough, working hard enough, working too hard, worthy. And managing it all. I tend to throw everything into what I'm doing, go hard, then crash and burn once every few months into a messy emotional heap that can only be resurrected with a few days of downtime and sleep. Then I get up again and go full tilt again!

# Mel's ADVICE

- Find what it is you love to do. Don't do it for money or status. It's important to feel challenged, stimulated, satisfied and useful.

- Foster a good support network. Partners, parents, friends, neighbours, babysitters; you honestly can't do it alone. And sometimes a Sunday morning walk or a Friday night glass of wine with your best friend is the best thing you can do for your mental health. You've also got to ask for help when you need it. It's a sign of strength not weakness.

- Finally, don't try to do everything. I don't think the term work/life balance is accurate – I say work/life priorities, because they change. My twenties were all about marriage, career and mortgage. My thirties were babies and work. Now in my forties I can carve a bit of time out for me, and I can take on other professional challenges I wouldn't have had the courage to twenty years ago. And I have got better at saying no. I've learnt it's okay to be honest and say you can't be there on that day.

# EMMA JANE PILKINGTON

INTERIOR DESIGNER

*Emma Jane Pilkington is an internationally recognised tastemaker and interior designer. Emma's polished yet eclectic style has been celebrated in publications such as* ELLE Decor *(A-List),* House and Garden, The New York Times *and* Vogue *to name a few. Based in Greenwich, Connecticut, she is called upon by clients across the world for her sharp eye and impeccable taste.*

I never planned to be an interior designer. Ever since I can remember, I always wanted to be a fashion designer. In Australia, as a little girl, I would devour American and French *Vogue* and obsess about what to wear on the one 'free' day of the year when we were not required to wear our strict English school uniforms – wool blackwatch tartan in the sweltering Sydney heat!

After college, I interned for American couturier James Purcell on Seventh Avenue in New York. I had spent the previous summer at Parsons (fashion school) and I assisted a stylist, working backstage at some great shows. It was the era of Kate Moss, Marc Jacobs and grunge. I loved it all. I have always had a strong interior dialogue in regard to aesthetics. It is my perpetual visual escapism. I moved on to fashion editorials until an illness side-tracked me. It was then that I fell into interiors.

I remember the day, it had started so well. It was August and I was on the beach in the Hamptons when my sister called. She told me that she had recommended me for an interior design job in Manhattan. My heart skipped in one of those moments when you know that your life is about to change. I was hired and shortly afterwards, the contractor left and I had to learn on my feet. I spent all my free time visiting showrooms, antique stores and fabric houses, poring over interior design books – I could not get enough. When you bounce out of bed with excitement, you must be on the right course.

In the beginning, I read and re-read Rose Tarlow's book *The Private House* as well as *Dwellings* by Stephen Sills and James Huniford. There was an attitude and an intimacy in them that hooked me. I responded to the light, the juxtaposition of the old and the new, and the subtle hand of a fabric. I wanted to live in these rooms. I wanted to create those rooms! As I studied historical periods at night and worked with top artisans during the day, I also honed my instinctual sense of space and scale. Seeing a project come together was exciting. I derived great pleasure from the smallest detail. With my innate ability to read a space and to envision how to furnish it, I realised that a career in the field could actually be fun!

The flip side to being creative can be the human element. I am by nature an introvert and as such, I find strength in solitude. In the beginning, I found learning how to navigate the client relationship to be rewarding and inspiring but, at times, it could be taxing. I lived and breathed a project, and with excitement also comes disillusion. I taught myself to be more detached and this has served me well.

**BUILDING SUCCESS**

My interiors are not scripted, rather they come from the gut. Perhaps my work has been successful because people respond as they would to a sincere conversation. I personally design each project so there is never repetition. I made the decision to keep my business small so I could continue to work in this manner. I need to be able to completely submerge myself in a place, sort of like an actor living a role. I am also proud and honoured to have been recognised within the industry. It still thrills me to be included in certain company, on various lists. A legendary talent once wrote me a note congratulating me on my work and I have kept it close to my desk ever since.

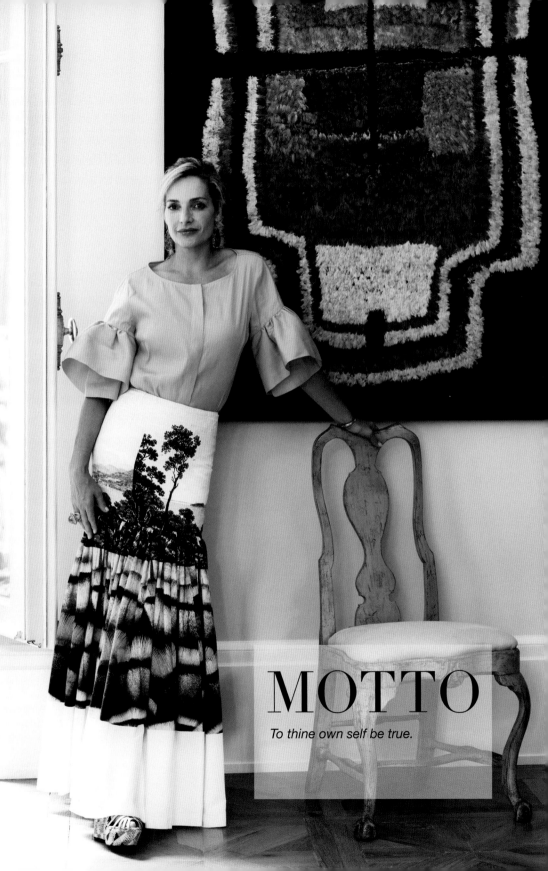

# MOTTO

*To thine own self be true.*

When I started my business, success was supported through editorials. Today, success is linked implicitly to social media. Being a private person, to date I have resisted the call. I am tempted, but it is a Pandora's box that I am still hesitant to open. I have enjoyed an organic success in both media and I have been fortunate to have done so without the need for self-promotion.

## INSPIRATIONS

My first mentor was my mother. Wherever we moved in the world, she had an amazing ability to create a beautiful home. Her rooms are just perfect. She has been my design partner and backbone from the beginning. We started working together when she moved to New York. We share a similar aesthetic and I can trust her responses implicitly. We also have great fun! I adore our days working together.

One of my earliest champions was Cynthia Frank. Larger than life, Cynthia was then an editor at *House and Garden* (how I miss that magazine!), and she introduced me to Dominique Browning, the Editor in Chief. Between wonderful editorial coverage and inclusion in the inaugural Tastemaker list, they really helped launch my career. For that, I am eternally grateful.

The most exciting people I've worked with were actually a team of brilliant designers and producers. I was asked to design the Moët & Chandon marquee at the Melbourne Cup. It was to be based on the Hall of Mirrors at Versailles. I worked remotely from the States with an incredible team in Melbourne. When I arrived there, the marquee was even more perfect than I could have imagined. I was born in Melbourne and the welcome that I received was very touching. This was a particularly exciting project for me.

Throughout my career, I have certainly had projects that get cut short or clients that disappoint me. Fortunately, another opportunity always comes along and my energy gets restored.

# Emma's
# *ADVICE*

- Identify your passion, feed it and commit to it 100 per cent.

- Do not take a break until the foundation is strong.

- Learn from others and be humble.

# DEFINE SUCCESS ON YOUR OWN TERMS, ACHIEVE IT BY YOUR OWN RULES, AND BUILD A LIFE YOU ARE PROUD TO LIVE

**ANNE SWEENEY**

# MOTTO

*The healthy life is the*
*only way. A rested body*
*is a healthy body.*

# JESSICA SEPEL

BESTSELLING AUTHOR, NUTRITIONIST

*Jessica's approach to a healthy lifestyle is informed by a well-researched understanding of nutrition and complemented by a passion to achieve physical and psychological balance. Her approach to health and nutrition aims to inspire people to live the best possible lifestyle by maintaining a healthy relationship with food and themselves.*

I was in a bit of a slump before I started. I wasn't exactly living the best life. I was partying too much, waking up incredibly anxious, a chronic fad dieter and buried in low self-esteem. Life didn't feel so good. I was very disconnected to my own body. I studied health and nutrition for five years, and learning about the body in such an in-depth way was my trigger to change. I was starting to understand that I wasn't treating my body very well. I started making healthier choices and created space for balance in my life – and my body (and life) starting healing. I created a blog to write about how I was healing and the healthy recipes I was discovering. My intention was to help as many women as I could who were going through the same struggles as I was. At the beginning, the biggest challenge was feeling worthy of the success of the blog. The blog became popular quite quickly and something I find challenging is overcoming self-doubt – I am working on it! Nowadays, I feel success is waking up every day, feeling fulfilled in my personal and business life. Waking up and being able to look forward to my day – this has got to be the new definition of success!

## THE HEALTHY LIFE

I think the biggest challenge has been healing myself and turning my life into something I love. I also feel so proud of all the people who have come along with me on my journey and embraced the healthy life; it is an achievement that I share with my community.

Nowadays, I am continually inspired by my community and patients from my nutrition clinic. I am constantly inspired by their desire to change/heal and embrace a healthier life. Their progress is incredibly inspiring. My mum has always been the best healthy cook I know. She taught me what it means to eat real wholefoods. My grandmother is also an incredible health role model who has inspired me always with her healthy way of life.

## THE JS HEALTH COMMUNITY

I am very in touch with my community – I listen to them. I watch their comments on social media and read all the emails I receive to make sure the advice and recipes I put out to them are in response to what they're needing. For example, I will receive an email from someone asking for more main meal ideas – and then I will know to create more main meals on the blog. It has been a challenge to stay honest, because being honest means you're open and vulnerable.

I started the blog as an outlet to keep a record of my own health journey as I studied nutrition, but I never expected it to become what it has today – so that's why it's so important, but sometimes a little difficult, to keep it so personal. Sometimes, I can be my own setback – I can be incredibly hard on myself. Being a perfectionist is a setback at times. It makes you feel you are not doing enough. Acknowledging all that I have done and created helps me overcome that.

# *Jess's* ADVICE

- Be authentic, be real – being real is relatable. If you are an aspiring blogger, have a powerful message that you know will resonate. Don't be afraid to share your story.

- Focus on your work not others. Keep your eye on your stuff. Don't compare yourself; it is a waste of time. That is a setback.

- Dream big. No more limits. Know you are worthy of success. I talk a lot about this in my books and blogs. You have to work on knowing your worth and believing you are deserving of success.

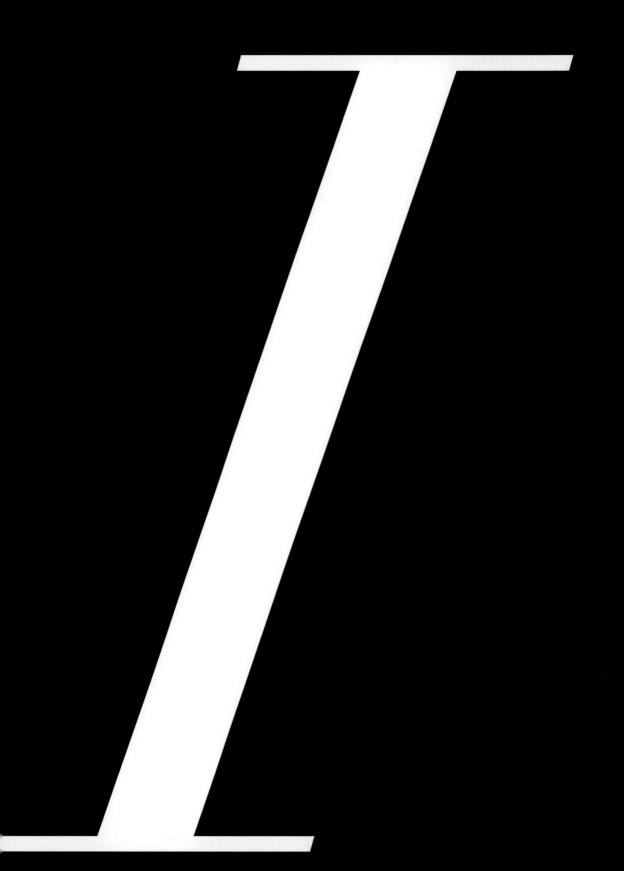

*IF YOU ARE*
*SUCCESSFUL,*
*IT IS BECAUSE*
*SOMEWHERE,*
*SOMETIME, SOMEONE*
*GAVE YOU A LIFE*
*OR AN IDEA THAT*
*STARTED YOU*
*IN THE RIGHT*
*DIRECTION*

MELINDA GATES

# MOTTO

We all have time, skills, and resources to do
something to make a difference in the lives of
others, even if it's something small. My life has
been changed forever through my experiences
working in Uganda – seeing children and their
parents strive for a better life. I believe in giving
– you get back tenfold!

# ANNABELLE CHAUNCY

## CEO AND FOUNDER OF SCHOOL FOR LIFE FOUNDATION

*Annabelle Chauncy was just twenty-one years old when she co-founded the School for Life Foundation in 2008 with the aim of empowering the children of Uganda by building schools that give quality education, while reaching out to the entire community by providing healthy food, clean drinking water, healthcare and employment, changing thousands of lives every year.*

"I was really lucky to grow up in small communities throughout my childhood. I am a country girl who was born and raised on a sheep and cattle farm in a small rural town called Canyonleigh (in New South Wales). I had four kids in my class, twenty-six kids in my primary school and my mum was my teacher! I then went on to a beautiful high school called Frensham where the motto was 'In Love Serve One Another'. There was a strong service ethos and giving back was a big part of the school's programs. We used to participate in the Duke of Edinburgh's International Award, Meals on Wheels, visit elderly in aged care facilities and do fundraisers for international and domestic charities. I was always driven to help others around me, particularly those who were suffering. I don't like inequality and I always found it hard to fathom that the luck of where you are born would have so much impact on the life and future you would have.

I went straight from school to university, without taking any time off study. I was seventeen and didn't really know who I was or what I wanted to be, but I got the marks to study Arts/Law at Sydney University and thought I wanted to work internationally with the

United Nations or as a journalist so I knew this degree would set me in good stead.

In 2007, I took six months off study at the age of twenty-one and travelled to Kenya and Uganda to teach English to children. When I got to Africa, I couldn't believe how many kids don't have the opportunity to go to school, and for those who do, how dire the learning conditions are. More than 100 kids would be crammed into a mud hut to learn, with no shoes on their feet, no uniforms, no desks, pens or pencils, their teachers may not even have any qualifications, but still they would come with a fierce determination and desire to learn because they knew that education would lift them out of poverty. I was so inspired by their drive and value for education, and I knew that it takes very little to make a difference in their lives, so decided that I wanted to build some schools. Never, at that time, did I know what a few schools would become!

**CHANGING THE WORLD**

Battling through my law degree, I was trying to find purpose in the cases I was reading and trying to understand how I was going to use my skills and education to do something to make a difference in the world! I was just twenty-one when I started School for Life Foundation and half-way through my degree, so I didn't really have much world or business experience. I was mostly fuelled by passion and a desire to find a tangible solution to a very solvable problem.

The idea developed when I met David Everett (co-founder) in 2007 in Kenya. He was studying International Development and had a strong theoretical understanding of the delivery of aid and some of the challenges faced by aid organisations. Our skills and passions were perfectly matched. We both had experienced first hand the life-changing power of education in Africa, and we were both driven to do something to make a difference. My law degree helped with setting up the business, writing the constitution, pulling together a Board of Directors and the like and David's International Development background helped to formulate how we would deliver our projects on the ground. We were both united in our belief that aid needs to be administered from the ground up, working hand in hand with the local community from the very beginning.

We undertook a few years of research and development in Uganda – sitting, looking and really listening. We identified the way aid programs were being delivered and saw that grassroots developments, which empower local people to help themselves, are the most successful methods for long term social change. We worked with the local and national government as well as the Ministry for Education to make sure we were planning services that would be sustainable for the long term.

**THE FOUNDATION**

School for Life started off as a passion to provide quality education and we certainly do that.

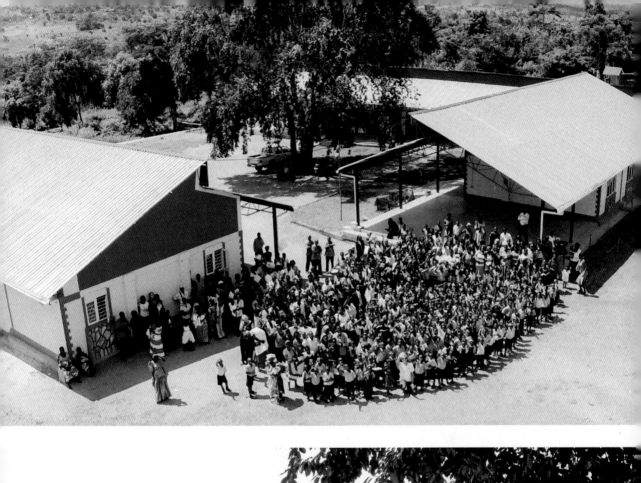

We provide 560 kids with education from pre-school to Year 7. We have also just built a secondary school and embarked on a third school, a primary school to continue our growth. We are on target to educate more than 1600 students within the next few years. But School for Life is not just about education, it's about building communities and serving them in a holistic way. We realised really quickly that the kids were coming to school and falling asleep on their desks everyday because they were suffering from such severe malnutrition. Their growth was stunted and they had fungal conditions on their skin. We provide all students and teachers with three nutritionally balanced meals, starting with breakfast each day. Then six of our builders came down with typhoid so we provided clean drinking water sources to the entire community. So the project unfolded, organically and holistically. We now have 120 local staff employed as cooks, cleaners, teachers, security, nurses, counsellors and builders. We educate more than 100 adults with literacy skills. We have trained and employed fifteen women as tailors to produce goods we market and sell in Australia, as well as all the uniforms for the kids and builders. We focus on agriculture, upskilling local farmers to get better yields from their land and we will grow our vocational school to incorporate carpentry, masonry, and a range of other contextually appropriate programs.

**UGANDA**

There were a number of reasons we chose Uganda. Firstly, it's politically stable and the Government openly supports investment in infrastructure, education and foreign aid. Statistically, there is an overwhelming need for education. There are 39 million people living in Uganda, in the state size of Victoria, Australia. Fifty-six per cent of them complete primary education. The life expectancy is just fifty-three years. The statistics are so much worse in rural areas, however, education is truly valued. Parents understand that education is freedom for their children and will struggle to afford them the opportunity to go to school.

There are so many additional challenges, though, once they get to school. In Uganda, the curriculum is taught in English, despite there being more than 150 different dialects spoken and very few speaking English at home. Children often have to walk 10 kilometres to get to school, on an empty stomach. Most children have only one meal per day, at night, and it lacks nutrients to help them grow and concentrate, thus leading to malnutrition. Whilst the government declares education to be free, there is a backlog of unpaid teacher wages from ten years ago, so teachers charge the parents a fee to teach their children. Many parents are subsistence farmers, living hand to mouth and so don't have the means to pay for their child's education.

Despite all of these challenges, I was drawn to Uganda. It has a vibrant positivity and generosity I've not seen before in other places. The local people would welcome me into their homes and give me the sweet potato they were going to feed their entire family for dinner, because they value hospitality and making people welcome. They find true joy in sharing. And that joy grew in me. They say the more give the more you get, and I really felt that. I was inspired to help, to do something small to make a difference to the lives of the Ugandans.

## GETTING SUPPORT

Our age stood in the way at the beginning when we were trying to drum up support to start the foundation. I remember a lot of people told me to come back to them when was grown up. I was fiercely determined though, not letting any of the naysayers or the critics deter me from carrying out my goal. I found some incredible business mentors who helped me formulate a strong business plan. Our Board of Directors were pivotal contributors as well, bringing credibility through their years of professional experience. Then we aligned with Rotary Australia, which was amazing. A sandstone organisation partnering with us helped enormously. I think the hardest part was pitching with a piece of paper showing architect drawings of an unbuilt school in Uganda because many people believed it was impossible to pull off.

The first project was land acquisition (10 acres), then the construction of two classrooms, ten drop toilets and enrolment of eighty students, with four teachers, in a foreign country, which is in some ways lawless. This was the start of the school. We knew from the beginning we needed to engage local leaders and staff to build and run the project, so relationships with the community were pivotal. The first wing of the school opened on 31st January 2011 – one of the highlights of my career. Eighty bright, happy little people attending school, who otherwise would never have had that opportunity. We also installed a borehole to give the entire community access to clean drinking water for free which was a great way of integrating into the community as everyone got some benefit from the school even if their kids weren't able to attend.

We now provide solar electricity (only 1 per cent of Ugandans have access to electricity) and implement environmentally sustainable programs where we can, including bio-gas toilets that convert waste to methane, and the methane is used for cooking meals. We have two health clinics and full-time nurses to serve the community's medical needs. We take the kids on excursions outside their community, and enrich their education with drama, art, music and dance.

In everything we do, we implement it, we analyse it and we try to make it better. It's a work in progress and it's grown faster and more successfully than I could ever have hoped.

## THE CHALLENGES

Being a female in business in Uganda is challenging – negotiating a patriarchal and at times corrupt environment to get the business off the ground.

In Australia, building the business and ensuring there are enough funds raised to support the growth has been challenging. Charity is a competitive space in Australia and there are so many competing, worthy causes out there. Sometimes I wake up in the middle of the night wondering how we are going to make our budget year on year and continue our life changing work. And then letting go in many ways has been a challenge. I am a perfectionist and growing a team means you need to

build trust and instil responsibility in them. It's hard to let go of your baby but I know that if I don't, it can't grow. We all make mistakes, but I think so long as you learn from them, it's not a bad thing.

Our biggest success I feel has been changing the lives of thousands of people in Uganda and equipping them with the skills, knowledge and resources they need to break free from the cycle of poverty. Education cannot be taken away so it's the greatest, longest lasting gift you can give someone. My greatest success has been opening the schools and ensuring that the flow on of their services and impact is to the entire community, not just the children.

I look to many people for inspiration; I am lucky to have met the most incredible people throughout my career. My dear friend Turia Pitt is a huge inspiration to me. I love her grit determination, her unwavering commitment to push on, despite tremendous hurdles and set backs. My mentor Professor Nadia Badawi AM is also such a role model, leader and support. Her commitment to School for Life and my success has been unwavering and I am indebted to her for the time she has dedicated to making me a better leader.

# Annabel's ADVICE

- Don't overthink it. I think if I had have given starting School for Life too much thought, I may have been too scared!

- Passion is an amazing tool, and if you can harness that passion for good, then even better. You want to wake up everyday doing something you truly love and that inspires you.

- My final advice is to go for it, be bold, be brave and be determined.

# MOTTO

*Go for it.*

# KAREN BEHNKE

## FOUNDER OF JUICE BEAUTY

*Entrepreneur, businesswoman and founder of Juice Beauty, Karen Behnke has managed to smash right through the glass ceiling and prove that some women really can have it all.*

My career began at the age of twenty-two, right out of college and I've enjoyed a long and successful entrepreneurial career in the Healthy Lifestyles/Sustainable sector of business. My consistent goal has been to marry my passion for helping people enjoy healthier lifestyles with building financially successful businesses that are mission driven.

My first company was an aerobics exercise company where I secured an army contract to teach fitness for various divisions of the military. That led me to starting one of the first corporate wellness companies in the country where I delivered worksite wellness to major corporations throughout the Western United States – pretty much before 'wellness' was a word!

I sold my wellness company to PacifiCare (now United Healthcare) and became their second female executive during the parent company's five-year growth phase as the company went from $1 billion to $5 billion in revenue. While I was having babies, I served on a few boards including 24 Hour Fitness during a seven-year growth period, turning it from $75 million to over $1 billion in revenue. This path all led to starting Juice Beauty!

## THE EVOLUTION OF JUICE BEAUTY

Experiencing hormonal changes and the beginning of lines in my skin in my early forties while I was pregnant with my two kids, I set out to find healthy skincare solutions that delivered visible results. I was astounded to learn that, although the skin absorbs over 60 per cent of what is placed on it, there were very few available healthy personal care products that worked well. So I literally became obsessed with the idea of creating beauty products with organic ingredients and wanted to create meaningful change in the beauty industry.

Years after my second child was born, I bought the name 'Juice Beauty' in 2004 and launched the company from scratch the following year. I set out to do the impossible: to create organic and natural formulations that perform as well as conventional beauty products, yet never compromise on the luxurious experience. Over the last several years, I have worked with PhD chemists, physicians, and microbiologists to perfect Juice Beauty's chemistry.

The brand's revolutionary formulations started with a basic premise: I believed that by formulating with an antioxidant and vitamin-rich organic botanical juice base, rather than petroleum derivatives or added water, and combining it with powerful skin care ingredients, it could yield equal or better results than conventional or natural products. Multiple clinical testing proved this premise to be true. Juice Beauty now has over 100 skincare products, all made with certified organic ingredients, yet is formulated to compete with high efficacy conventional chemical brands. It was a natural progression to move into makeup with the same quality and organic ingredient standards.

## THE COLLABORATION WITH GWYNETH PALTROW

Gwyneth Paltrow and I were introduced by a mutual investor and the collaboration came together because of our shared values. I wanted an authentic business relationship with a celebrity that would fit the eco-authenticity of our company – we have ten abiding eco-values: sourcing certified organic ingredients, sourcing many ingredients locally from the West Coast, utilising solar power for some of our manufacturing, no animal testing and more. After an initial great meeting with Gwyneth (over organic chicken salad) and discussing our shared values, we quickly agreed that we could form a partnership to

# Karen's
# *ADVICE*

- Follow your passion.

- Trust your gut.

- Marry someone who is supportive of your entrepreneurial personality.

create a great makeup collection with Gwyneth serving as Creative Director of Makeup. We both wanted luxurious makeup products but without any of the potentially toxic ingredients. Additionally, Gwyneth really wanted to develop products that had conventional chemical efficacy and application and vibrancy, not just the typical sheer natural products. Real makeup with high-power, high-payoff pigments that could stand the test of the red carpet.

Gwyneth worked alongside me and our scientists and our product development team for several months, choosing all of the packaging, the colour ranges, the final textures and she also named all of the products.

## THE CHALLENGES

The biggest challenge in the beginning was changing the way beauty chemistry was done. Formulating with organic botanical juices using such high quality plant-based ingredients was a new concept, so we were really experimenting with groundbreaking and new formulations. It was extremely difficult to match the slip and feel of silicones and dimethicones and all those plastic things that are included in conventional beauty products, but we eventually did it with organic grape seed jojoba and shea.

With conventional chemical makeup, it's easy to use synthetic dyes to get the colours, but you can imagine how hard it is to use plant-based colours from crushed roses and aubergine for our Phyto-Pigments makeup made with organic ingredients. It's tough to match colours as nature doesn't always produce the exact same colour each time!

With people, in the early days of Juice Beauty, my biggest challenge was attracting an experienced team of professionals and now, fortunately, we have an incredible group of beauty executives as well as in-house chemists, a fabulous Creative Director of Makeup, Gwyneth Paltrow, and overall, just an incredible team. Juice Beauty's skincare products started selling really well at about our fifth year when we brought in a professional in-house chemist and product development team, upgraded all of our product formulations and recruited an experienced management team. When we were able to achieve the same slip and feel with organic grape seed, jojoba and shea as conventional chemical brands do with petroleum PEGS, silicones and dimethicones, we started doing really well. It goes back to the products (they must be great!) and people

(our internal team and our customers).

In addition, the partnership between Gwyneth Paltrow and Juice Beauty has helped enormously on account of her worldwide fame, how she is instantly recognised and most importantly, in the way Gwyneth is an authentic proponent of my lifelong mission to make wonderful clean beauty formulations available to the world. Awareness of Gwyneth Paltrow will continue to bring greater awareness to Juice Beauty and I hope also in general, to all healthy beauty products made with organic ingredients.

My family and both of our kids and my husband (cardiologist by day, thinks about Juice Beauty by night) are very involved in thinking about the business and helping when they can. That is one of my biggest achievements: successfully meshing my business and personal life because as an entrepreneur, it's a necessity!

**INSPIRATIONS**

My team, as well as our customers, inspire and motivate me daily. I really draw inspiration from this incredible group of employees, as well as reading our customer comments and attending to our in-store events, and interacting with customers.

Gwyneth and I share the same attention to minute details with formulas and packaging, so it was inspiring to see the same level of dedication with the development of the makeup and skincare collections with her as I have shown myself for the past ten years. Gwyneth and I are both working mothers and we both share a passion for health and wellness through exercise, nutrition and now beauty. Seeing in Gwyneth the mutual goal of filling the white space in the market for healthy, high-performance makeup made the launch of the new Juice Beauty Phyto-Pigments makeup an exciting project along the way.

I also had the opportunity to lead the development and produce Goop by Juice Beauty, a luxe skincare collection made with certified organic ingredients, which is the first Goop branded consumer goods ever created – the perfect alignment of the shared vision of Gwyneth and me. I also really enjoy working with Mary Dillon, who leads Ulta Beauty, such a high growth, publicly held and amazing retailer led by a fabulous woman.

## OVERCOMING CHALLENGES

Formulating Juice Beauty's Phyto-Pigments makeup has been very challenging and actually achieving such amazing quality with our mascara has been a miracle!

Gwyneth and I were adamant about not having any endocrine-disrupting artificial dyes in any of the makeup formulas, that they are vegan (so no animal glue or beeswax either, of course) and no petroleum-derived ingredients like carbon black. It is much harder to create makeup without having any recourse to synthetic colours and petroleum-derived ingredients.

Having the makeup products last on your skin and look vibrant throughout the day with plant-derived ingredients and formulas that are made with certified organic ingredients is no easy task. But I am personally proud to say that Gwyneth and I created seventy-five formulas together in the space of a year, all made with certified organic ingredients, and all of them were matched to a conventional makeup/skincare benchmark that Gwyneth provided and never once compromised on performance.

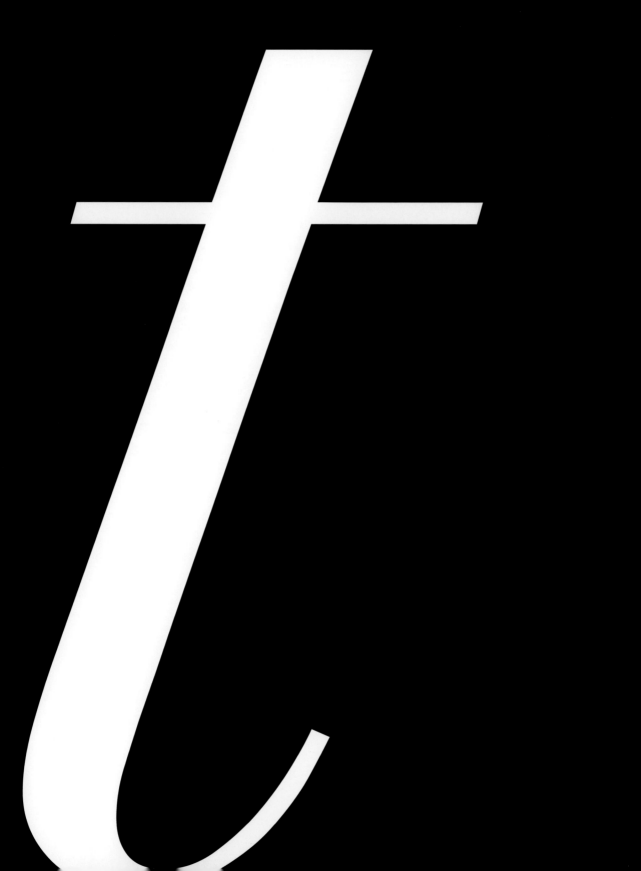

*THE ONLY WAY
TO DO SOMETHING IN
DEPTH IS TO WORK
HARD. THE MOMENT
YOU START BEING
IN LOVE WITH WHAT
YOU'RE DOING
AND THINKING IT'S
BEAUTIFUL OR RICH,
THEN YOU
ARE IN DANGER*

**MIUCCIA PRADA**

# PHILIPPA POMERANZ

PRODUCER, DIRECTOR, AUTHOR

*Philippa Pomeranz runs her own successful production company which develops and produces television and film both in the United States and Australia. She is the co-creator and executive producer of* Fashion Bloggers, *an Australian television show that has gone global.*

I think I was always destined to be in my career, but it took me a little while to realise that doing what you love can become your career. To understand my journey, I have to go back to my school years. I went to an all girls school, in an affluent part of Sydney. In my spare time, whilst everyone was playing sports, and in between my ballet and dancing lessons, I would make short films as birthday gifts. I would write poetry, short stories and direct little plays or music videos starring my friends. I think I was producing from the beginning!

However, when I left high school, I felt completely lost. I knew I wanted to do something creative, but I couldn't figure out how I could turn my passion into a profession. I didn't know how to get a foot in the door, especially because I had spent so much time dreaming over my poetry and short stories instead of studying, so my grades really suffered. Remember there was no Google or social media at that time either.

There were only two film schools in those days: one in Sydney and one in Melbourne. I applied to both but was rejected by both on the grounds that I needed life experience, so I reluctantly enrolled in graphic design school. I graduated from there and decided to jump on a plane and head to England. No one was going to stop me from pursuing my dream. I had butterflies as I walked through customs alone, but I was on my way! For the next two years, I embraced the culture and absorbed as much as I could. I went on European adventures and experienced the world in ways that I never imagined. My heart and vision had changed forever.

It was during this time that my parents decided to move to Los Angeles from Sydney for business reasons. It was just the opening I needed and I knew I wanted to be there too. It was my destiny to attend film school in the heart of the global entertainment industry and nothing was going to stop me. Within a week, I was packed and on my way to LA. I was selected to attend the highly regarded USC School of Cinematic Arts. It was a major turning point in my life as it allowed me to learn not only the craft of film making, but also the business of the film industry. I don't believe in being a starving artist!

After graduating from USC (who said I didn't have academic prowess), my first job was in Los Angeles at The Style Network on a reality show called *You're Invited*. We shot thirteen episodes in a season with a small team, which allowed me to find my feet across multiple disciplines and work quickly through the ranks. There were many exhausting hours on set as well as late nights in post production – and I loved every minute. I remained in LA for thirteen years and these experiences in television proved invaluable when the time came for me to create my own content. I still remember that moment I decided to start my production company. It was 5 a.m. and I was driving down Laurel Canyon after a long night on set. I had Dido blasting and I excitedly thought it's now or never!

My production company Core3 Entertainment has just celebrated its tenth birthday and has an array of television and film projects in development and production both in Australia and the USA. I'm most excited about directing my first feature film, so watch this space!

# MOTTO

*I'm only a day away. This is really important to my fluidity. It means that anything is possible because I won't let distance stand in my way.*

**FASHION BLOGGERS TV**

The TV show *Fashion Bloggers* was born out of curiosity. Blogging was a world I knew very little about. It's a world where girls are dominating. Bloggers have a huge social media reach which means there's a built-in audience – a major plus when pitching a new television format. Casting is all about authentic friendships and relationships, along with girls with relatable and aspirational stories to tell.

The *Fashion Bloggers* cast is ever-changing because digital influencers are always on the move, but our Fashion Blogger family remains supportive of each other.

**OVERCOMING OBSTACLES**

I think that the biggest challenge has been finding my place in the world and gaining confidence. I have the most loving, supportive family who always encouraged me to chase my dreams. But ultimately, it was up to me to go for it. I think that's why I have such a strong work ethic and never take what I do for granted.

Working in a field that I love is so important to me. I know people say this all the time, but you just can't beat that. Networking and building relationships is so vital in my field, plus sheer determination and self-belief has contributed to my ongoing success. Sometimes, people are asked if they weren't doing this, what would they be doing? My answer is this: I'm working in a field I love. I'm passionate about getting up in the morning and going to work. I love that everyday is different.

It's also very important to maintain relationships even when you get knocked down. They will say 'yes' one day. Truthfully, it's incredibly hard to get projects onto to the screen in my industry. It is all about persistence and not taking no for an answer. I know I'm not going to win every battle, although I would like to!

# *Pippy's* TIPS

- Get on with it, and don't be afraid to learn from your mistakes. You are the author of your story; the creator of your destiny, so don't let anyone tell you no. #ladyboss #girlpower

- Set goals, not only professional goals, but personal ones too.

- Don't be afraid to learn from people older or younger than you. *Fashion Bloggers* is the perfect example, it's been incredibly rewarding, not only because of its success, but it keeps me up-to-speed on the ever-changing fast-paced digital age.

- Work in an industry that you love. For me, it's never been about the rewards but about the product I create: be it television shows, films, books or a brand like 'The Umbrella Girls'. I want my work to reflect me. I want to inspire, empower and encourage women and girls around the world to chase their dreams just like I have. You can have a happy, awesome life when you do!

# MOTTO

*What doesn't kill me, makes
me stronger ... and funnier.*

# CAMILLA CLEESE

## COMEDIAN

*Camilla Cleese is a comedian, writer and actor, currently residing in Los Angeles, California. She is the daughter of famed comedian, John Cleese, and is a former model and equestrian.*

It's hard to pinpoint exactly when my career in comedy began. Growing up, I was surrounded by comedians and received an invaluable education without realising it. Strangely, I had never really considered pursuing a career in comedy; in part this was because at some subconscious level I think I was afraid I wouldn't live up to the family name, escape my father's shadow, or more importantly, make him proud.

I began riding horses at about eight years old, and by the time I was a teenager it had become my life. I always thought I would ride professionally, but after I attempted to defer university for a third year, my father intervened. In retrospect, I'm glad he did, as I am still dealing with the repercussions from the countless injuries incurred. Should I have continued, I probably wouldn't be walking anymore. So, I attended the University of California, Santa Barbara (sometimes ... Not as often as I should have!) and hoped to find something I would be passionate about. I worked side jobs, internships, in restaurants, event planning and hotel management, but nothing seemed like a fit. My attitude didn't help either and I have a hard time taking things seriously, especially people who take themselves too seriously, and found many of those industries didn't appreciate a smart ass who takes so much joy in playing pranks.

One day, I went to see a stand up show with a friend. One of the comedians was hilarious, relatable, my age, and a girl— something I had never seen before. Her name was Sarah Tiana. Seeing someone similar to myself was the first time it occurred to me that I could actually, maybe do stand up. And I wanted to do it; I wanted to get really good at it, like her. It's crazy to think that I had made it to that age without really being aware of the possibility. I went up to her after the show and we became fast friends. A few months later, with some help and encouragement from Sarah, I took that first step onto stage at an open mic, and the rest was history.

## THE CHALLENGES

My biggest challenge has been overcoming fear. Fear of failure, mostly. Bombing is one of the worst feelings in the world. But after a while you learn that even the best comics have bad nights, and if you can figure out what went wrong you can turn your mistakes into learning opportunities.

Learning to take risks has been an important part of success, and not to be afraid of making mistakes. Especially in stand up, talent will only take you so far. It takes a lot of time and hard work, day in and day out, if you want to have any chance of success. Tenacity is key, you have to want it more than anything because the personal sacrifices are great; I said goodbye to my social life, my boyfriend, and have missed countless holidays and events because I work most nights. Also, you have to be strong and thick skinned, especially as a woman.

## A MAN'S WORLD

New comics face a certain amount of hazing, both on stage and off, and the women get the brunt of it. Unfortunately, there is still rampant misogyny in the stand up world. Not everywhere though, some clubs are less tolerant of it than others – but it is widely accepted and, in some places, encouraged. One experience I had early on changed how I dealt with those experiences, and thank god, because there have been many.

When I first did a set at the open mic at an LA comedy club, I was only a few months in, but actually did quite well considering. After my set the MC came back on the stage and said to the audience, 'Well, that was mildly entertaining… for a woman. But who cares – by round of applause, how many people would fuck that chick?' I was hurt and furious, and went back to my car in tears. As I sat there, I remember deciding that I had to channel all that anger and frustration into being a better comic so I could prove

# Camilla's
# *ADVICE*

- Never give up.

- Don't be afraid to
  make mistakes.

- Rejection is an inevitable
  part of the journey
  to success.

- Give zero f---- about what
  other people think of you.

that stigma wrong. Being more successful and funnier than the guys who behaved like that would be the ultimate revenge. It is satisfying to know that their attempts to hurt me, or any of my girlfriends in comedy, actually drove me to be better.

The stigma that women aren't funny still lingers in all the rooms, despite the massive success of some of the incredibly talented comedians – Sarah Silverman, Whitney Cummings, Natasha Leggero, Chelsea Handler, Amy Schumer, Nicky Glaser and so many more – and yet it is perpetuated. There are no overnight successes in stand up.

I have been so fortunate to be able to learn from and work with my father – I couldn't ask for a better mentor when it comes to comedy! All the female comedians who have paved the way before me, particularly Tig Notaro, Natasha Leggero, Sarah Tiana, and Kathleen Madigan have definitely been inspirations. But most importantly, my mother has been instrumental in my career. She was the first to suggest I do stand up, years before it became a reality – I only wish I had listened to her sooner. She had an amazing sense of humour and was my biggest supporter. It breaks my heart that she never got to see me do stand up live, but I always feel she is with me in spirit.

*KEEP YOUR EYES OPEN, BECAUSE WHATEVER YOU CAN SEE CAN INSPIRE YOU*

**GRACE CODDINGTON**

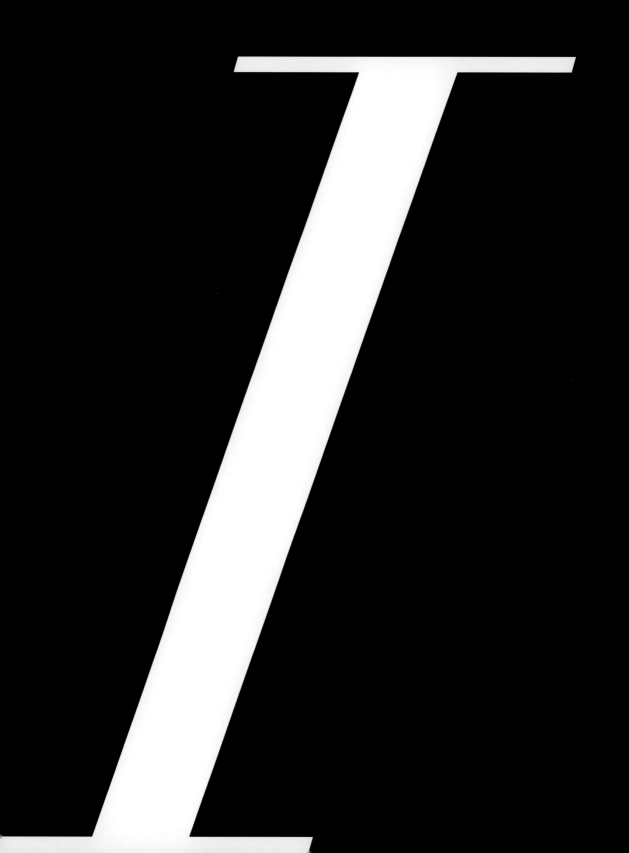

*I LEARNED TO ALWAYS TAKE ON THINGS I'D NEVER DONE BEFORE. GROWTH AND COMFORT DO NOT COEXIST*

**VIRGINIA ROMETTY**

# MOTTO

*Proper planning prevents poor performance – so true with everything you do!*

# REBECCA WILLIAMS

## FOUNDER OF BECCA COSMETICS

*After a successful career as a makeup artist in Perth, Western Australia, Rebecca Morrice Williams was frustrated by her inability to find the perfect foundation. After six years of scientific research and development, she founded the BECCA Cosmetics line, which has now evolved into a cult beauty product sold around the world. The brand has recently been purchased by Estée Lauder.*

For as long as I can remember, I've been in love with fashion and magazines, and obsessed with makeup, cosmetics and skin. I bought all the fashion magazines I came across and wondered about the apparent flawlessness of the faces of the models on the covers and throughout the fashion and beauty spreads. I grew up believing that foundation was the answer to perfect looking skin.

Even as a young girl, I was an avid consumer of cosmetics, spending all my pocket money and any free time in chemists and cosmetic department stores – trying and buying all the different types of foundations and concealers and then experimenting on myself later. I had periods in my life where my skin was fantastically clear, and other times when I had blemishes. At those times (when the skin is not perfect), the foundation you use is put to test. I became increasing frustrated with the formulations and colours that were available in the marketplace at that time. The textures were either too heavy or too light, and the colours were not yellow enough for my own skin type. They were all too orange or pink toned. The result was a mask-like finish – skin that did not look natural and a face that did not match the neck and chest of the user. In my opinion, the perfect foundation did not exist!

As a makeup artist working in the '90s (before any significant digital retouching), I became known in Australia for very clean-looking makeup and creating the best-looking complexions. Working in both fashion and with 'real women', I realised that the needs of the photographic and catwalk model was far different from the needs of real women. However, they all wanted the same result – perfect skin.

At this time, I had begun to mix textures and colours, and had developed a way of applying products to create the most natural-looking finish for variable skin types. There were products or aspects of products that I liked from different brands (including theatrical, commercial and corrective brands) – but nothing that was a foolproof system with colours for all women. And there wasn't a makeup brand that made its focus just on foundation.

## BRAND BECCA

For two years I worked unsuccessfully with a local chemist who really did not have the expertise in formulating makeup. After explaining my business idea to my friend and mentor Steven Schapera, he agreed to partner with me and to financially back the project in its infancy – that was 1996. Steven was a winemaker and marketer, and saw similarities between the wine and cosmetic industries. His scientific, technological and business background was the perfect skill set to match my creativity and vision.

Whilst still working in our respective day jobs, we travelled overseas to find a manufacturer with the expertise and technology that we were after. From 1996–2000 we developed the core BECCA products (foundation, concealer and powder). During this time, I tested my samples on around 1500 women.

The normal product development process for a new brand in this industry would have been to source one of the big contract manufacturers, choose a base formula and change some aspect (i.e. fragrance or colour). However, I chose to innovate by describing the end point first and working with my manufacturer from scratch in order to meet my list of criteria for the product. This made the development times longer and created more risk.

In 2000 a company was incorporated to bring the BECCA brand to commerciality, and the development of the colour range continued.

From the start it was my mission to give every women on the planet the products to enable them to achieve a perfect complexion, so there was a lot of development work in formulating the colours – and as the foundations also included SPF, this added some technical hurdles.

Armed with a selection of laboratory samples, mock-up visuals of how the package would look, details of the philosophy of the brand, the Skin Perfecting Makeup System and conceptual campaign visuals, the brand was received very well and accepted into two of the world's premier retailers – Space NK and Bergdorf Goodman.

## GOING GLOBAL

We launched with Space NK (United Kingdom) in October 2001 and in Bergdorf Goodman (New York) in January 2002. Fairly quickly we received glowing editorial support from the press and with two such high profile retailers carrying the line there was a lot of interest from other retailers and acceptance into our home market – Australia.

Launching into the UK and USA before our home market was fairly different to what most companies would do. You are always told to build your brand and learn your lessons at home before moving on to conquer the rest of the world. It was our specific strategy to build our brand overseas first in order to gain acceptance at home. This was at a time when Australia was not as confident in being proud of its own talent unless they had been accepted elsewhere. (It is quite different now, though!)

Over the years the brand has evolved and our marketing strategy has evolved. What started as a fairly small business run out of Perth, Western Australia, and shipping to various stores across in Australia, USA, Europe and Asia, has now become a large business with its headquarters in New York.

What has made BECCA unique from the start was its focus on the complexion. Today, the brand is known as an authority on complexion and experts in the beauty of light.

## SPEED BUMPS

The biggest challenges in the early days was mainly to do with having enough money – for enough stock, for great staff and for the sort of marketing required to support the brand and get it to stand out amongst other high profile and very well known brands.

We were very lucky to get high profile makeup artists and celebrities to use the brand right from the beginning, so this all flowed through to lots of great editorial in magazines. This then lead to increased interest from new markets and stores looking for new and unique cult brands.

# *Rebecca's* TIPS

- Follow your dreams and be passionate about what you do!

- Try to identify a gap in the marketplace for a product or brand – usually from your own needs. You can identify what is lacking or has not been done well enough.

- Network with other women to see if this is in fact a need other women have.

- Make sure your product or brand looks, feels, and is different from what is already in the market. If possible, have a marketable story behind it. You have to set your self apart – it is the only way to compete in a saturated market.

- Know exactly who your target customer is and don't try to be everything to everyone.

- Ensure that the product or brand can have longevity and is more than just a product. Make your brand unable to be copied by giving it a distinctive personality.

# MOTTO

*Be unstoppable! In approaching challenges and setting up a new business, you have to be brave and really believe in what you're doing – you have to be an unstoppable force.*

# CHRISTIANE DUIGAN

### DIRECTOR OF BODYISM

*The Bodyism system is the blueprint for a long, lean, healthy body, created by A-list personal trainer James Duigan and his wife, Christiane (known as 'Mrs Clean and Lean'). Together, they are helping clients around the world become lean, strong and glowing inside and out.*

I grew up in a family that owned a business, and so by osmosis I picked up the knowledge on how to run a small business from going after school to help out and doing odd jobs for my parents. When I completed my education and entered the workforce, I didn't really know what I wanted to do. Having grown up in Australia playing sports and living a heathy Aussie lifestyle, I knew I had an interest in health and wellness. I tried multiple jobs, from valuing jewellery to working on a shop floor, and in the course of these experiences, by default, I grew my business knowledge. I learned about operations, marketing, finance and human resources.

I always came back to my interest of health and wellness. You could always find me trying the newest gym class, on every fad diet and trying all the new restaurants. It wasn't until I met James who introduced me to the Clean and Lean way that I was able to make sustainable and profound transformations in my body and mind, so I knew it really worked.

**BODYISM**

Bodyism was a method that James came up with for a long, lean, beautiful body. It has evolved throughout the years but continues to change people lives through movement, breathing, thought and nutrition. It helps to empower the individual to make the right choices for themselves to change their lives. I met James when he just founded Bodyism; it was a small personal training studio in Chelsea. I then put all my previous experience and skills from working in a small business into practise by doing anything and everything – like invoicing clients to putting flowers in the bathroom. His vision and passion to share his message, combined with the fact that it changed my life, helped me to quickly get involved and grow Bodyism into what it is today.

At Bodyism we were never trying to fill a market gap. Instead Bodyism came about because we wanted to change people's lives. We wanted to provide a solution that was safe, results driven and sustainable for life. For us, it's all about the 'why' – we do it to help change people's lives. All of the other arms of our business have really sprung from that goal. Therefore it was never a challenge getting it off the ground because of the integrity and authenticity behind it. We have, however, faced challenges within the business once it was off the ground, and that has been around building the right team. We have been so lucky with the amazing people we have worked with but there are sadly those few who will do things to get in the way of its success. Still, we choose to be unstoppable, no matter what happens. That is the difference between a business that makes it and one that doesn't.

We never expected the health and wellness market to blow up like it has. It's very exciting that it is now such a growing industry. While it's wonderful that so much attention is being paid to health and wellness, you do have to be so careful about where you get your information from. There are a lot of new people in the market making claims that have no real credibility. Luckily, we are placed as a 'sane' voice that is all about balance and being kind to yourself and others, so the method has never been a fad. It's had constant steady growth throughout the years, which is why I feel it is so successful. We are also constantly evolving and growing ourselves to make sure we are at the forefront of new ideas and methods.

We are so grateful for everything we have achieved in business from our Clean and Lean diet books to our flagship cafe and concept store in Notting Hill, and couldn't

# *Christiane's* TIPS

- Follow your own instincts! No one knows your business better than you.

- It is of course important to get advice and speak to people about their experience, wins and mistakes – but then gather the information you need to make the best decisions for your business.

- Never give up. Things often get in the way, people try to bring you down and things go wrong, but you can never give up.

- When you make a mistake you have to own it. Pick yourself back up, and don't do the same thing again.

have done it without the beautiful people around us who were supporting us to make things happen. But my biggest achievement definitely has to be giving birth to our two gorgeous children, Charlotte and Leonardo. They are the biggest joy in my life and make me completely fulfilled. It was the best and most real experience of my life, which was completely life changing.

## THE FUTURE

Nowadays a typical day for me involves taking my kids to school, then heading to the club to take meetings – usually on new business – and catching up with my team. I enjoy a delicious lunch from the Clean and Lean café, always making sure I have my favourite Beauty Food smoothie. Afternoons may involve editing our new book or new product development. Then when I can, I squeeze in some ballet at the club with Karis, one of our wonderful ballet teachers.

  We also have an amazing and ambitious investment partner who is supporting us in our growth to different parts of the world like America and the UAE, which we're very excited about.

# MOTTO

*As one of the most successful young women of this generation said, 'Being fearless isn't being not fearful, it's being terrified but you jump anyway.'*
*– Taylor Swift*

# SOPHIE FALKINER

## MODEL, TV PRESENTER

*One of Australia's most recognisable faces, Sophie Falkiner is a television presenter, model and spokeswoman for various charities.*

I was twenty-one years old, lying in a hospital bed, hooked up to various machines, my lungs draining of fluid with new 'hardware' fused to my spine, when I had an epiphany: I did not want an average life! Perhaps it was the morphine speaking, but I felt more inspired than ever before. This wasn't about amassing a fortune, seeking fame or celebrity status. It was about new adventures, getting to know people from all walks of life and embarking on a rich and varied career. A desk job just wasn't going to cut it!

I understood in that moment that personal adversity both galvanises and invigorates change. Also, with passion and dedication you can find your true calling. So it began; a university degree, four part time jobs, free work experience, a ton of networking and knocking on countless doors. It was not long before I realised that with a positive attitude, confidence, discipline and some good old fashioned hustle, you can achieve more than you dared to dream.

I didn't have an 'in' in the television industry, a family member who preceded me, or even a famous last name. I wasn't the most beautiful in a casting situation or even the smartest. What I did have was fearlessness, determination and a self-deprecating sense of humour.

The flow-on effect amazed me. I was suddenly on a network show airing five times a week; my dream gig as a travel reporter travelling the globe, becoming an entertainment presenter and interviewing interesting and diverse people. MC gigs, charity work, numerous ambassadorial roles for the likes of clients such as Wonderbra and Neutrogena followed. Plus, financial independence.

## BEING A GAME CHANGER

What I have learned is that it's important never to give up and to always remain relevant. Also, connect with other female mentors and seek out positive role models. Keeping yourself up to date, informed and prepared to learn new crafts and technologies is pivotal to long term success. Also, do not be afraid to ask for that promotion, salary rise, holiday or even a helping hand. Often it's as simple as 'ask and you shall receive'. Never let change scare you. Be fearless. Sometimes option A might not work out, but option B might be a hell of a lot more successful, not to mention satisfying!

An important personal lesson was not to lose my identity or sense of self in a man or with motherhood. This is very difficult, especially when your unconditional love for your children overwhelms you. I had to remind myself never to stop learning, challenging and occasionally scaring myself.

Complacency doesn't promote positive change, growth or personal prosperity. Another life lesson was to always keep my own bank accounts, hobbies, passions and friends, as long term these will serve you well.

Mastering the art of 'balance' is a perennial problem many women face. This has also been one of my greatest challenges! Quentin Bryce, the former Governor General of Australia, once said, 'You can have it all, but not at the same time'. I totally agree. Something usually has to give when women are in either full work mode or full mummy or relationship mode. The key is not to lose yourself during these periods.

Realise that life is about timing; your day will come. So keep investing in yourself regardless of if you are covered in baby vomit and you haven't showered in days!

Don't be the woman who forgets her passions and what inspires her because she is so wrapped up in the feeling of 'being in love' that she invests all her energies into her partner and not herself. This might sound a tad controversial, but I believe that it is often when we are single and solely focused on our career, perhaps with fewer 'balls in the air', that we can accomplish the most.

I strongly suggest being a little selfish sometimes. Trust me, men do it all the time! I constantly strive to be proud of myself and my achievements, and also to be a good role model for my children.

# Sophie's TIPS

- My life to date has had its ups and downs. I have been tested many times and I have also had to go to Plan B more times than I care to count. I have enjoyed many career and personal highs. However, having resilience and treating people how you want to be treated yourself has served me exceptionally well.

- Integrity and knowing who you are amongst the crowd and surrounding yourself with good people are also hugely beneficial.

- Don't be scared to take that leap of faith and back yourself. Be genuine and accessible.

- Listen. As a leader your own values should match those of your business.

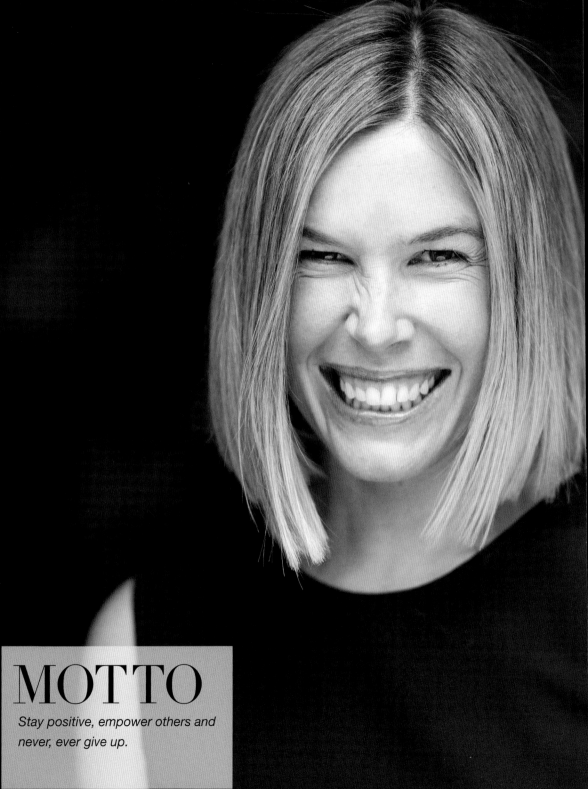

# MOTTO

*Stay positive, empower others and never, ever give up.*

# BIANCA MONLEY

FOUNDER OF EAT FIT FOOD

*The founder of food delivery service Eat Fit Food, Bianca Monley pioneered the healthy meal delivery market fifteen years ago. She continues to dominate the market with constant innovation and passion for the business she started from humble beginnings in her own kitchen.*

Before I started Eat Fit Food, I was working at Fitness First Health Club in Sydney's Eastern suburbs carrying out Membership sales. While working in the fitness industry, I became disillusioned when I saw what people were eating and what their perception of healthy food entailed. From that moment on, I recognised a gap in the market and decided to take action!

I started Eat Fit Food in 2002 when I was just twenty-two years old. My vision was to produce incredibly tasty, nutritious and fresh home delivered meals packed full of natural produce. I am truly passionate about food and fitness, and believe that eating well and feeling healthy should be an enjoyable part of everyone's daily life.

**THE PHILOSOPHY**

Eat Fit Food was started to make a difference in the way people feel through nourishing food. We have found having healthy food dropped at your doorstep makes it so much easier for our time-poor customers. We decided to do a delivery service as I wanted to reach as many people as we could and not be restricted to certain areas, with a view to expand worldwide. In the beginning, I was living in a small apartment based in Bondi.

As the business experienced some growth spurts, my weekends quickly turned into me rushing off to the fresh food markets on a Sunday morning, buying produce, bringing it home to prepare and then cook on my grill. I recall having to cook outside on the balcony many times as it smoked out my apartment!

After packing the food into individual containers and cooler bags, I would go to bed and get up at 3 a.m. to start my delivery shift, so all of my clients would receive their cooler bags by 7 a.m. that day. Soon enough, more orders were flying in and I bought my first van and then set up a commercial kitchen.

## THE CHALLENGES

In the early days, it was extremely difficult to get funding as the banks wouldn't go near my start-up and I didn't have enough collateral to offer them as insurance. So thankfully, some friends stepped in and helped me along the way. Starting a new business is extremely hard work but also one of the most rewarding things you can do. For me personally, not having previous business experience was a huge lesson and I definitely learned the hard way. Usually by making some rash decisions, which resulted in me losing more money than I intended to.

However, on the flipside, by making

## Bianca's *TIPS*

- Never give up. No matter how hard it becomes, stay positive, express gratitude and challenge negative thoughts.

- Define your business goals both long-term and short-term. The most important rule of goal setting is honesty. Confront your decisions with confidence as this will result in greater success.

- Write a business plan. What you plan to do and how you plan to do it. Close your eyes. Imagine that it is three years from now, where do you want to be?

- Find a mentor or business coach, someone you admire and look up to.

- Manage your cash flow from the very beginning. Cash flow is the lifeline of your business. Grow organically, but always keep in mind the following: know your break even, maintain a cash reserve and collect your receivables immediately.

these mistakes I learned something new and began to take the business to the next level. Staying strong and believing in yourself is key. It is also important to surround yourself with positive people who will elevate you and provide you with the ongoing support you need.

## THE SUCCESS OF EAT FIT FOOD

Technology has played a huge part in the success of the brand. Having a functional website where people can order their meals and programs online within a few clicks of a button is real time saver. Social media has also made a huge difference, from brand awareness, understanding our audience, getting instant feedback from our customers' perspective, generating leads and creating meaningful relationships with like-minded brands.

Another key to the success of Eat Fit Food has been staying utterly committed to our core beliefs. Our strength is providing our clients with premium quality meals and produce, as well as first class customer service. We believe in the long-term view and we do not sacrifice our fundamental beliefs.

My family has always been a big support through all the ups and downs. My parents set me up early in life to work hard for what you want and to always believe in yourself and never give up. Also, being surrounded by uplifting positive people, my health, my family and fabulous food.

Eat Fit food has my heart and soul, utterly and completely. I call it my first-born child as I had the opportunity to build it brick by brick from scratch myself. However, over the past three years there has been a slight shift due to me having three beautiful children. Therein lies my biggest challenge, trying to do it all! Being a mum, wife and boss each day and wearing multiple hats, has you going in so many different directions and striving to be your best each and every day.

## BUSINESSWOMAN AWARD

My biggest achievement so far is winning the Veuve Clicquot Business Woman Award in March 2016! The Veuve Clicquot New Generation Award is part of a global initiative, and recognises the success and vision of up-and-coming entrepreneurial business women, specifically those under forty years of age. This age group has been selected as it correlates to the formative years of Madame Clicquot's own tenure at the House. Madame Clicquot was just twenty-seven years of age when she took over Veuve Clicquot Ponsardin following the death of her husband.

I was chosen by the panel of judges as the young female entrepreneur who best reflects Madame Clicquot's values of innovation, audacity and fearlessness. Like Madame Clicquot, the panel recognised me as a true innovator, identifying a market opportunity for healthy home-delivered food over a decade ago and staying ahead of the curve as the segment has exploded in recent years.

When I heard about the award, I was extremely grateful. I had never imagined I would ever receive an award of this calibre and it made me sit and recognise what I have actually achieved over the years to get me to this nomination.

As a business owner, we are always tasked with creating new and exciting business ideas. Winning this award made me appreciate the journey I have been on for the last fifteen years and recognising the path I've forged in changing so many people's lives for the better.

It has also opened up so many doors for me including business relationships and connections. I have now formed a wonderful relationship with my now mentor Maryanne Shearer, founder of T2.

# MOTTO

*Live generously. Be generous with your thoughts, your words and your actions. When I'm at work, I always try to be generous in my service to customers, generous towards my business partner and generous towards my team. Generosity bounces back around you.*

# LIBERTY WATSON

## FASHION DESIGNER

*Liberty Watson is one half of the talented duo behind Sydney-based label Watson X Watson, taking the Australian fashion scene by storm by creating beautiful, sophisticated, quality clothes and shoes.*

Before I began my career in fashion, I was a singer. I was signed to sing at five-star resorts on Friday and Saturday nights. Then I sort of fell into fashion, working for a company where my sister was working at the time.

We spent six years learning the ropes of the fashion industry and running a fashion business for our boss, who lived overseas at the time. We worked really hard and treated it like it was our own label. My sister and I grew that company from five wholesale stores to 120, with two department store accounts, and suddenly I realised, hey, we might be good at this!

## THE BEGINNINGS

I was twenty-eight and I had just sold both of my properties. I'd always wanted to start my own business and now we had the experience. So finally, with a nest egg of money in the bank, it felt like the right time. My sister, Somer, and I work really well together and have quite different skill sets, so it made sense to work together again. And that's when Watson X Watson came to life.

# *Liberty's* ADVICE

- Believe in what you do. We always believed in what we were doing. It takes so much energy and hard work to make it in the fashion industry or in any business. There are tough days and on those days you really see what you are made of. You either get creative and make things happen, or you give up. We really gave it everything and backed it with our life savings.

- Put all your energy behind it, have a clear focus and set goals. If you have a business partner, being unified on all fronts is crucial.

Of course, there have been so many challenges along the way. There really are days where you feel like giving up, but I'm glad we pushed through. For us, one of the most difficult parts has been other people letting us down. The fashion industry was experiencing a lot of bankruptcies and liquidations when we started out, so often we found ourselves paying off their mistakes – as they would keep our stock and close their doors. There were a few hard hits that were out of our control. To recover, we sometimes had to work six or seven days a week, but we got there in the end!

## BUILDING THE BRAND

Working as a team always creates a fun energy. With the same goal, you really can achieve anything. We are both really hard workers; our parents definitely instilled a really hard work ethic into us from a young age. We've also invested a lot into our product. We always purchase the very best materials and produce everything locally so the quality is really beautiful.

## EXPANSION

We quickly worked out what we were good at and stayed true to our style, which includes luxurious staples and the pieces that are the backbone of a woman's wardrobe: that leather mini, stretch leather pants, a perfectly fitted shirt, a beautiful cashmere coat, a structured dress that fits like a glove – the items that you want to wear over and over again, and keep forever. We make sure everything we create is essential to a woman's wardrobe and we make clothes that will last the distance.

Creating a brand that women are madly in love with is an exciting thing. We realise that we aren't saving lives here but the clothes bring so much joy to the people who buy them and makes them feel good, and that's a pretty positive thing. We are also really proud of our Fashion Week runway shows. Seeing the story come to life on a runway is very rewarding. We work tirelessly on our shows and at the end of countless hours in the sewing room, when it all comes together, it is so wonderful to see it all, and you really feel you have kicked goals. Eventually our dream is to create a menswear line too!

*SOMETIMES YOU DON'T ALWAYS KNOW WHERE YOU ARE GOING, BUT IF YOU DO WHAT YOU LOVE THE PATH WILL BECOME MORE CLEAR*

**STEPH ADAMS**

# MOTTO

*Never give in, never give up and
never take no for an answer.*

# SHELLEY SULLIVAN

## CEO AND FOUNDER OF MODELCO COSMETICS

*Hailed as one of Australia's leading entrepreneurs, Shelley Sullivan is an innovator and leader. She single-handedly created the international cosmetics empire ModelCo in 2002, and grew it into the much-loved beauty brand it is today, celebrated by women across the globe.*

I always had a strong desire to create my own business – the feeling was innate in me from an early age. I love a challenge, love being creative and love the thrill of building a business I can be proud of. It all started when I was working at a modeling agency as a receptionist. I was looking at the way this particular agent managed his talent, and I looked at myself and thought that I could open my own agency and provide personalised service. I started my own modeling agency at twenty-one with one model who wasn't even tall. She was about 5 foot 5, but she was gorgeous! I figured for photography, no one really knows how tall you are. Over the duration of ten years, we grew to 1200 talents across four different categories: editorial, advertising, children's models and actors.

I was continually listening to what my models wished they'd had in their beauty regime. And they often complained that all the luxury brands weren't providing what they really needed.

Eight years into my talent agency, I loved what I was doing, but I felt like I needed a change of industry. I felt like doing something more innovative and on a global scale. I have always been obsessed by beauty products and noticed a gap in the market within the premium beauty brands.

## HOW MODELCO WAS BORN

My models used to come in with these red blow dryer burns on their eyes. I asked them what it was and they said they were trying to curl their eyelashes. They were heating their old-style eyelash curlers with their hairdryers and then applying hair spray! So I thought; wouldn't it be amazing if I could create this innovative blow dryer for the eyelashes?

I did extensive research, and discovered that South Korea was the best place at the time to create gadgets. So, I jumped on a plane. I thought it was going to be easy! We were driving through the backstreets of Korea and ended up at this manufacturer. He thought I was insane when I came in withall of my drawings and said, 'How do you create this?' He said we could make these all from scratch, but that I needed to buy a minimum of 3000 units. To me that was a huge number, but I really believed in the concept. Having belief and knowing it's something that is going to sell is extremely important. I launched Turbo Lashwand into Australian retail with staggering results. I sold thousands of units in one month. It was huge. It was at that point that I didn't look at the profit, but I realised that there is a need in the beauty industry for innovative beauty products. I knew that if I could continue a whole range of products in the beauty, cosmetics and tanning category, which women really wanted, that I was onto something big.

Looking back, I can attribute the success of the brand to three things: the sheer innovation of the products, celebrity endorsement – Kylie Minogue and Elle Macpherson said that they loved the Turbo Lashwand and Tan Airbrush in a Can – and the fact that we launched it in a Fashion Week and secured editorials in beauty magazines, giving it credibility in the industry.

## STAR POWER

I have always cultivated relationships with celebrities – I believe in my products, and it is affirming to know that high profile women do too! I was lucky that my background in managing talent gave me inroads to high profile celebrities and I was able to gift them products. Past celebrity brand ambassadors include Elle Macpherson, Dannii Minogue, Cheyenne Tozzi, Rosie Huntington-Whiteley and our current brand ambassador, Hailey Baldwin. It was difficult at first, to fulfill the sheer volumes of orders I was receiving! I was not used to ordering stock and managing distribution. I thought I was going into the world of beauty, but in reality, I was going into the world of wholesale, retailing, logistics, financing, PR and so on. It was also challenging to expand internationally to countries with a language and cultural barrier. In terms of my biggest success, that is definitely a toss-up between launching Tan Airbrush in a Can and signing Hailey Baldwin. I was sick of looking at my models coming in with orange streaked legs, and just knew there had to be a smarter and more user-friendly way for women to self-tan. I had often thought about the idea of marrying self-tan with a spray bottle. I knew that if I could create a product that put an end to stained hands and uneven coverage, that it would be a success!

When Tan Airbrush in Can – the world's first airbrush 'tan in a can' self-tanning product – hit the market, it truly changed the way woman self-tanned, delivering professional results with the convenience of an at-home application. It truly transcended convention and has since been copied by some of the world's biggest cosmetic companies.

Collaborating with Hailey Baldwin to launch the Hailey Baldwin for ModelCo collection was a major coup for ModelCo. First and foremost, our ambassadors have to genuinely love the brand and our products. We create products for style savvy yet time poor women who want to look and feel fabulous. Not only is Hailey

## Shelley's *ADVICE*

- Understand the business that you are going into.

- Surround yourself with people who have more knowledge than you and who can guide you through the process.

- Work out the funds you need to start up and then double them!

- Trust your instincts – they have never failed me before!

stylish, sophisticated and glamorous, she's also an internationally recognised model and US It girl who truly encapsulates those values and attributes. We love that Hailey makes everything look so effortless and glamorous and she appeals to the mass millenial audience. That's what ModelCo is about – achievable, everyday glamour.

# I'VE ALWAYS BELIEVED THAT ONE WOMAN'S SUCCESS CAN ONLY HELP ANOTHER WOMAN'S SUCCESS

GLORIA VANDERBILT

# MOTTO

*I am responsible for*
*my happiness.*

# KAREN FISCHER

AUTHOR, NUTRITIONIST, TV HOST, FOUNDER OF JOLIEE SKIN

*Former television host Karen Fischer is a certified nutritionist and product innovator. She is the award-winning author of five health books and her regular clientele spans from Australia to New Zealand, United Kingdom, America, Canada and Dubai. With her passion and interest in nutritional biochemistry, she designed a diet and an eczema supplement that cleared up her daughter's eczema and has helped people around the world.*

I'm not quite sure why I'm so determined to make something of my life; to work long hours and forego a normal social life. It's possibly because my mother always believed wholeheartedly in me. Even when I made bad decisions, she never cautioned me to be sensible. Sometimes I wish she had! I have made many mistakes that at times cost me dearly and humbled me greatly. I guess my mistakes have helped me to be more discerning, to trust my instincts, make better decisions, look after myself and be kinder to myself.

Before I began writing books and launched Joliee Skin, I hosted an Australian TV program on the Nine Network called *What's Up, Doc?* At the time, I was eating unhealthy food, I had skin problems and I felt tired and moody. So on my days off from filming, I studied to become a nutritionist. The job in television enabled me to buy a house. However, I didn't appreciate how great my life was, and I ended up with no house in favour of being self-employed, earning little money and following my 'big' dreams, which took a decade longer than expected.

## FOCUSING ON SKIN

Several factors influenced my decision to focus on treating skin disorders. During my teenage years, I felt constantly embarrassed about my skin breakouts and severe hand dermatitis. I would hide my hands, which would bleed whenever I washed them. I briefly had psoriasis over half of my body, so being healthy became an essential part of my life.

Another great motivator was my daughter. Soon after her birth, she developed eczema. By the time she was two, she was growing resentful about being different from her friends. Her skin was incredibly itchy. Overnight she would scratch it while in bed and would wake up in the morning with blood on her sheets. She had many food sensitivities and allergies, including dust mite allergy. She had to give away her fluffy toys! So I vowed I would help her lead a normal life.

With the knowledge that I had gathered, and a lot of extra research, I developed a supplement and food program for my daughter. Soon, she had beautiful skin! That was more than a decade ago.

Since then I have prescribed the product to my patients. Now after years of research, testing and planning, the products are available online and in pharmacies, which is a dream come true.

## THE CHALLENGES

I've had many challenges and I still do. Running a clinic and a supplement company while raising two children on my own is quite a juggle. However, I've hired great people to help run the clinic and Skin Friend.

If I were to give advice to other women I would say: positive thinking is good but it can get you into trouble. Rather than repeating the mantra, 'I will be successful', do a lot of research on the market you are investing your time and money into. Ask yourself, is it is a growing industry or a dying one?

Is there a place in the market for me and do I offer something different that people want and need? Be honest about your talents and work on them. Also exercise and eat healthy food, as they create true positive feelings. Get help with financial forecasts, don't risk your house for any business and be a realist as well as a dreamer. Failing to be practical can leave you in debt so don't brush practicality aside.

Writing books and our Facebook page were instrumental in our success. As a result we had a large online eczema community waiting for the products to launch. We also had a lucky break when our products were featured on 7 News. However, helping people who are suffering is, and has always been, my number one goal. The best reward is hearing customers say, 'My child no longer has eczema!'

# Karen's
# *ADVICE*

- Begin with a good, sound idea.

- Choose branding that you really, really love. This can take longer than expected (we rebranded several times before launching). Good branding may also save you a fortune on marketing, so don't let anyone talk you into choosing a design or branding you don't love.

- If you are in the depths of despair (we've all been there), you might like to take a break and have fun with supportive friends and family. Then get back to making your dreams a reality.

*WAKE UP.*
*BE KIND.*
*WORK HARD.*
*BE FEARLESS.*
*REPEAT*

**SAMANTHA BRETT**

# ANDREA HORWOOD BUX

CO-FOUNDER OF WELLECO, FOUNDER OF INVISIBLE ZINC,
CREATOR OF AUSTRALIAN STYLE MAGAZINE

*Creator of multi-award winning magazine* Australian Style, *Andrea Horwood Bux is a true Game Changer. She created a breakthrough chemical free sunscreen in the bestselling Invisible Zinc. Her latest venture with supermodel Elle Macpherson brings us the worldwide phenomenon of wellness company WelleCo and The Super Elixir, a specialised alkalising greens supplement which aims to help people around the world to improve their health and vitality, and find their beauty within.*

I started *Australian Style* magazine when I was nineteen years old. At the time in Australia, most magazines were owned by two publishers and the independent landscape didn't really exist. There was an exciting, young wave of talent in Australia, we were all looking to London for fashion and music and the magazines that grew from this like *Face* and *iD*. We had nothing like it in Australia and we were hungry for something of our own. So we created it.

I started *Australian Style* as more of a talent co-operative that turned into a business. I like to believe *Australian Style* was a great cadetship for that young talent. We were a brave, independent title with a free agenda and an open door that encouraged a lively exchange of arts, fashion, architecture, design, music and literature – everything that was in our world of interest. It was also a rich training ground for many who populate the top-end of fashion and publishing in Australia today.

At *Australian Style* we produced all our own original material. This was my rule to ensure that we could have a valid voice and see things our way. Perhaps this made us a truer documenter of popular culture of the time. It also meant everyone we interviewed had to spend a fair bit of time with us – from the biggest international bands to the coolest reclusive artists and poets. And we had to spend time with them! (It made life very interesting, the school I loved to learn in.) This gave us a deeper exchange and formed our character as a magazine.

I also believe that popular culture should be written and documented by the people who are living it, so there will be a natural time to pass it on. I cringe a little when corporations try to talk to 'the kids'. So after nearly fifteen years, I felt it was time that I sold the magazine. I then went home to Western Australia and started Invisible Zinc.

## BREAKING BOUNDARIES

Invisible Zinc was a long and difficult road. When we launched, every sunscreen on the market was a chemical one. They didn't protect the skin the way our natural zinc did, but they were cheaper and were owned by the pharmaceutical giants – a bit of a challenge there.

First, we had to formulate with new technology to make the zinc creams wearable. It took many attempts to get it right. Then we had to communicate our message via the media because we had no advertising budget. We also had to earn shelf space across pharmacy, grocery and department stores – everywhere the chemical sunscreens were sold. I remember going back every year to the big grocery duos in Australia, only to be knocked back every time (I may have put my product in their Chairman's letterbox from time to time, asking why a better, safer sunscreen wasn't on their shelves!). In under ten years, we were able to make Invisible Zinc an iconic product across the country. Our technology is being used globally and will one day hopefully be the only form of sunscreen we use. But this didn't exist when we started – when a group of research scientists in the particle engineering department of The University of Western Australia first came to us to help commercialise their development. So, there was a lot of hard work behind that success that people don't see. I hope this helps illustrate what it takes between idea and the perceived fast success.

# THE SUPER ELIXIR™
## By WelleCo

THE
SUPER
ELIXIR

300g Net
Fine Powder
www.welleco.com

# Andrea's TIPS

- From publishing *Australian Style* to starting Invisible Zinc and now WelleCo, one thing has proved true for me every time: if you have a vision, something you absolutely believe in, then you have to work harder than anyone else and make it happen yourself, no shortcuts, no out-sourcing responsibility.

- Build your brand as fast as you can and make it famous (and I believe the brand should be famous, not you). If you have a great idea and execute it well, you need to grow *fast* so it can't be copied.

- Own your mistakes and learn from them; I made and still make many.

- Find good people and be open and inclusive, you can't do it on your own.

## THE NEXT BIG THING

After we sold Invisible Zinc, Elle Macpherson and I were in Sydney doing our final press week for Invisible Zinc when she said that next time we worked together she would like to be in business with me (until then, Elle was the face of our Invisible Zinc advertising campaigns and an early supporter). After seeing her in action during these long days, very early starts and dozens of press interviews, sailing through and looking so fresh and beautiful when I was in a heap by midday, I asked what was in the green powder she was taking every morning (my friends would want to know!). I learned about it, started taking it and believed strongly that this should be our new business together. The idea of high-grade bio-live food supplements (processed without heat so the nutrients are alive) as a modern upgrade to synthetic vitamins was compelling. So, after many months and formulation work between Elle's nutritional doctor in London and our Australian PhDs on the final formulation, The Super Elixir was born in March, 2014.

## BEAUTY FROM WITHIN

Our first product, The Super Elixir Alkalising Greens, is the foundation of the whole business and the reason WelleCo exists. It is also the most complicated and difficult to communicate: a green powder instead of a tablet, and why we should have a healthy alkaline pH level in the body for good health. Not exactly snappy sound bites!

We had the expected reaction from some of the British tabloid press early on; 'Expensive, looks like pond scum, just eat your veggies'. But we knew. We waited as more and more people tried it. They told their friends, bought it for their mothers and boyfriends and after a year or so the same tabloids reported that we had sparked a global frenzy.

The packaging is unique. We needed opaque glass to preserve the integrity of the bio-live ingredients and I have always loved and collected 1930s glass. So in the tradition of the ones I love – Rene Lalique for Guerlain, Karl Palda from Czechoslovakia – we commissioned Australian contemporary glass artist Jasper Dowding (who'd designed for the likes of Asprey and Saatchi) to design our beautiful black caddy, which is made by a French glass manufacturer and also preserves the integrity of the bio-live ingredients from UV degradation. Basically, I do believe in contributing something good. Since our launch we have become a cult product, available in over sixty countries and a favourite amongst celebrities and sporting personalities. Our aim was to create the world's best whole food and organic supplements, and with the addition of our all-plant Nourishing Protein, Sleep Welle Tea, range of everyday essentials and 'good to go' food, we are achieving this goal. The success of The Super Elixir comes down to the product, the team and all the people around the world who now take it every day and talk about it. That's what WelleCo is based on: goodwill.

## *Andrea's* TIPS

- You have to trust your vision and defend it doggedly. Everyone will have an opinion, your enthusiasm will be dampened and you will have many setbacks. Keep pushing through. No one fights hard for a bad idea, so it's a great proof test too.

- There are no instant successes. I can honestly say that nothing I have done has been easy.

- Even though you may be a mouse, you can still have giant ambitions!

*WE NEED TO MOVE BEYOND THE IDEA THAT GIRLS CAN BE LEADERS AND CREATE THE EXPECTATION THAT THEY SHOULD BE LEADERS*

CONDOLEEZZA RICE

# MOTTO

*Enjoy the ride. Life is short – too short to stress over the small things. In the end, none of it matters anyway, it is the way you feel, the experiences you have and the memories you make that remain with you forever.*

# VICTORIA CURTIS

## FOUNDER OF CURTIS COLLECTION

*Taking the industry by storm, award-winning makeup artist Victoria Curtis's own makeup collection is transforming complexions of women around the globe.*

"My love affair with all things beauty began at a very young age. I can attribute this to my mother, who was always dressed immaculately. Her hair and makeup were flawless and she never left the house without a beautifully made up face. This left a lasting impression on me and ultimately shaped me into the woman that I am today.

As a teenager, my very first job was in a hair and beauty salon; an environment that I grew to love. I recall watching with fascination as women transformed their appearance, and as a result built their confidence and self-esteem. My passion for the beauty industry was ignited during this time, and it gives me great pleasure to know that I can now offer women confidence-building products and solutions to their beauty concerns through the use of my cosmetics.

## THE EARLY DAYS

Following my high school years, I completed a double degree in Accounting and Marketing and went abroad to study in the United States. On my return, I was fortunate enough to be offered a graduate position at L'Oreal Australia in the Marketing Department of the Professional Products Division. This allowed me to once again connect with the salon and spa industry. I gained insight into the other side of the industry by offering support and business development programs to salon owners. I took a keen interest in the philosophy of these salons and what they were trying to achieve for their clients. It was during this time that I discovered a gap in the market.

I felt that there was an opportunity to launch a luxury cosmetics brand exclusively for the industry. My vision and point of difference was to combine the chic and style of designer cosmetics with the high quality, pharmaceutical grade ingredients that complimented a salon's services and acted as the final step in their clients' treatment plan.

## VISION TO REALITY

This vision came to life some three years later through my own research and development. I travelled the globe to source products, packaging and formulas that I felt were exactly what I would love to use and carry in my personal makeup bag. I also wanted the products to include the most powerful skincare benefits available on the market.

After testing the formulas on own skin, which I had battled with for years to keep clear, I discovered a formula that, in conjunction with my skin care treatments, allowed me to finally achieve results in the form of clear, glowing skin. The secret is in our vita-mineral infused formulations which are designed to feed your skin with antioxidants, offer SPF protection, hydration and nourishment, while delivering the most flawless finish due to the light reflecting minerals.

The Curtis Mineral Finish is best described as having the most complimentary lighting on your complexion all day long. We like to refer to it as the Curtis Collection 'Signature Candle Lit Glow': a soft focus finish that allows you to future proof your beauty by protecting your skin against age aggressors. Our message to young women is to be proactive and prevent the ageing process, rather than being reactive and have to then attempt to reverse it.

## OUR MESSAGE

Education is so crucial. I am personally passionate about sharing this message with women and offering them the information which they may not otherwise be privy to about their skin,

and the importance of using mineral cosmetics. This has now lead me down another career path (unexpectedly) as a key note/public speaker. This is something I enjoy immensely; it has allowed me to achieve personal growth and has given me the reinforcement that what we are doing is meaningful and resonates with woman who are seeking advice and answers for their beauty concerns. My goal is to offer a woman beauty solutions that can ultimately improve the way she feels about herself and her appearance. Whether she has battled dark circles all her life, redness in her skin or gaps in her eyebrows, we have carefully selected a collection of products designed to address these beauty concerns. This goes beyond makeup.

For me, it is about that moment when a woman looks at herself and genuinely cannot believe that she has found a solution to the one thing she has always felt self-conscious about. She immediately lights up and there is a sparkle in her eye and confidence in her smile that wasn't there before. This is why we truly believe that the Curtis Collection brand offers more than just makeup to woman of all ages.

## THE CHALLENGES

My biggest challenge is finding time for a work/life balance. As a start-up business, you ultimately are your business. You live and breathe it and you become invested in it in every way. As you should. It does consume me, however, at this stage of my life I would not have it any other way. We are in a huge growth phase and I am completely committed to that. My goals drive me to strive for excellence in everything that I do.

I am fortunate enough to have my husband involved in my business, which means that we can enjoy this incredible journey together. He is my partner in life, in business and my biggest supporter. Being a professional athlete (A-League star Michael Theo), his discipline, drive and achievements are inspiring, but it is his ability to overcome adversity that has really proved to me that, with belief and courage, anything is possible for anyone.

Passion and resilience are ultimately the key. We are all faced with challenges and setbacks, it is how we grow from these experiences and bounce back that matters. I am never discouraged by a 'no' or a door closing. Rather, I am grateful as it always leads me down the path and to the door that I am supposed to open.

## GROWING THE BRAND

In an industry dominated by big players, I have never let this intimidate me and what I am trying to achieve. I have never seen my competition as a threat, rather I have always felt that I might be a threat to my competition.

I do not spend time focusing on what anyone else is doing. I am true to my vision for the brand and what we stand for and I am committed to offering women more than makeup. I never deviate from this and I feel that this is the reason the brand has such a strong, loyal following.

I also attribute my understanding of my business to my university degree – the combination of marketing and accounting allows me to explore my creative side, with the restraint required to make smart business decisions. I have always had a 'big brand' mentality which assisted me in laying solid foundations for future growth and opportunities. I don't believe in luck, I believe in preparation meeting opportunity and the belief in yourself to take a calculated risk at the time that it presents itself.

I am proud to say that Curtis Collection is now an international brand. In total, Curtis Collection is now available at 300 retail locations across Australia and New Zealand, which is an incredible achievement in such a short period of time. I believe our strong brand values and commitment to our industry have contributed to this success. We have invested back in those who have invested in us and as a result we have allowed our partners to grow with us.

Our retailers are ultimately the faces of my brand and an extension of me. It is imperative that they share my passion and understand our brand message and what we are trying to achieve for our clients. For this reason, I train and educate my retailers personally and make myself available to each and every one of them. Communication is everything; without this, we lack understanding of our market and become disconnected to those who are ultimately dictating whether our brand is a success. I pride myself on listening and responding quickly. My father – who has worked on luxury brands for the majority of his professional career and is now holds the position of CEO for Porsche Cars Australia – has always told me that your brand is not necessarily what you believe it is, it's what your market perceives it to be. This key message resonates with me. It ensures that every decision I make is in the best interests of my brand and my customers.

We are honoured to be invited every year to sponsor some of Australia's most respected fashion designers at Mercedes Benz Fashion Week in Sydney. The exposure that this has given our brand has proved priceless and once again has contributed to our growth and brand awareness.

Our strong ties to the fashion industry are what inspired me to create the Curtis Collection Makeup Styling Guide in 2015 and pioneer the idea of makeup style. Fashion is all about style. It is about selecting a colour palette that is aesthetically pleasing on the eye by marrying complementary tones together. Makeup style is much the same. It determines whether our skin tone looks radiant or washed out; whether our eyes are bright or dull, and

## Victoria's TIPS

- Trust in the timing of your life. I believe that I am exactly where I am suppose to be. I dream big, but I know that there are steps that I must take to get there.

- The combination of patience, hard work and belief are the formula to success, achieving your goals and seeing your dreams become a reality.

- Confidence is essential, believing in the message that you have to share and what your brand stands for. I am confident in everything that I do, it excites me to share my passion with the women that I am fortunate enough to meet throughout my journey.

- Remove fear from the equation and shift your energy and focus on yourself and what you have to offer. This will naturally then attract the types of people who you should be working with.

whether our hair colour is vibrant or lacks brightness due to the fact that it is not matched correctly to our skin's undertones. The theory behind our new beauty concept is that if your makeup style is on point, this will inevitably bring your skin tone, hair and eye colour to life. The issue is that most women are unsure as to which colour tones compliment their skin tone and in turn bring attention their best features.

After months of development, colour selections and testing our Makeup Styling Guide was launched to the market with an overwhelming response from the media as well as our clients. The unique styling guide, which creates a wardrobe of makeup looks for the user by recommending their personal colour palette from the Curtis Collection product range, determines results by asking the user to select their skin shade, undertone, hair colour and eye colour. Based on our professional recommendations, the results are calculated and the user can shop their perfect matches in our collection! This one of a kind online tool is something we are incredibly proud of and personally one of my greatest achievements thus far.

# MOTTO

*Don't think, just do!*

# ALYCE TRAN

## CO-FOUNDER OF THE DAILY EDITED

*Established in 2011, The Daily Edited is an online store stocking an
innovative line of personalised leather goods, designed and created by Alyce Tran
and Tania Liu. With backgrounds in corporate law, these two women have created
a range of accessories that are practical yet chic at the same time. There is
absolutely no need to be drab in the office!*

I've always been in business, so to speak. My parents are quite entrepreneurial so
I was always setting up little things within their businesses, for example, I had a
strawberry stall at our front gate when my parents farmed and wholesaled
strawberries. I was eight years old at the time!

I started out my career as a lawyer. The day-to-day work, as you can
imagine, wasn't that thrilling and I have always enjoyed having hobbies on the side. The
Daily Edited began as an 'on the side' hobby, and just took off!

The Daily Edited actually started as a blog and mood board for things I loved that I
posted daily. Tania Liu (my co-founder) and I then had the idea to post and sell 'daily outfits'
on the site. So we launched our clothing label under the name 'Edited'.

After running this business for a year or so and facing various challenges that the
apparel business brings, we decided to pivot into accessories. I was actually shopping for a
few items that I could use for work one afternoon – like a laptop case and a compendium –

and I couldn't really find anything. Everything was either horrendously expensive or not at all chic.

I called Tania and said, 'We need to do something about this.' We launched with three products in three colours ways in September 2014 and haven't looked back since!

Getting the word out has been all about the product itself. I think our brand's profile has been growing as we have a product that is quite versatile and is suitable to a wide audience, allowing us to reach and strike a chord with a range of people, including well-known identities.

## BIG MILESTONES

There have been a couple of big milestones so far. The first was when Tania and I decided we could hand in our resignation (our business was making enough money to cover our lawyer's salaries effectively) to our respective bosses to work on The Daily Edited full time. And the second was when our brand was received by David Jones to be sold alongside so many other great brands!

Next was getting an investor on board. We actually never went looking for an investor, they came to us. I think if you are doing good things and your business is sound, then naturally people will be interested in coming on that journey with you and hopefully they will get a return on their investment.

# Alyce's
# *TIPS*

- If you have an idea just go with it, you never know where it might lead.

- The worst-case scenario is you lose a bit of cash, but you will learn so much!

*DON'T WORRY ABOUT BEING SUCCESSFUL BUT WORK TOWARD BEING SIGNIFICANT AND THE SUCCESS WILL NATURALLY FOLLOW*

**OPRAH WINFREY**

# MOTTO

*Put everything you have into everything you do.*

# AMANDA SHADFORTH

## PHOTOGRAPHER, INFLUENCER

*Amanda Shadforth is the founder of the world-renowned fashion site
Oracle Fox. She is also one of the stars of a successful fashion television series
which was featured in over 120 countries, and chronicles her journey as a
leading digital influencer.*

Before I started Oracle Fox, I had my own boutique art gallery. I was a fine artist working mostly in acrylic and oils, and was lucky enough to exhibit internationally. Art has always been a big part of my life and I feel like it was important for it to emanate through every touch point of Oracle Fox.

During days in my studio when I wasn't painting, I would spend my time searching the internet for inspiration and beautiful images. I needed an outlet for all the beautiful materials I was finding and started Oracle Fox as a personal mood board. Before long, I started posting my own images and focusing on my social media platforms. Everything has grown organically from this point. I think Oracle Fox was a natural progression for me as an artist and is a wonderful way to engage with a diverse audience as well as the creative community.

Managing the growth of Oracle Fox has been a challenge but it's also very rewarding. The industry is growing exponentially and I believe that it's key to stay one step ahead. I now have a full-time team and although the business side can be quite challenging, it's been a really positive experience surrounding myself with people who believe in Oracle Fox as much as I do. It sounds cliché but hard work and dedication have been essential, and it wouldn't be possible to stay so focused on my business without the support of my beautiful friends and family. I'm as focused on growing Oracle Fox now as I was at the beginning. I also feel that in this industry it's absolutely essential to embrace change and continue to innovate and evolve your brand; things change so rapidly and I always make sure I stay one step ahead.

The calibre of collaborations that we've creatively directed has just been incredible and we've been lucky enough to work closely with brands such as Louis Vuitton, Viktor & Rolf and Versace on separate digital campaigns. The quality of projects that we're involved with has been enabled by this platform we've created. It's amazing to think that something as vast as Oracle Fox has been built from just a single idea.

## THE FUTURE

There is no denying that Oracle Fox has taken me on some amazing adventure, and allowed me to realise many of my goals, some which were previously just a dream. I'm always humbled by this. My ultimate career goal is to continue to grow the Oracle Fox brand and to share beautiful original content with my readers. To be honest, my greatest competitor is myself, so I am always working on pushing through my own boundaries and limitations. This is a really satisfying process and serves as an ongoing challenge which is showcased through my work. Being a fine artist by trade, I have high expectations and I am extremely critical of my own work. I am passionate about my photographic and styling projects, and continually work towards the growth of Oracle Fox and the Oracle Fox Journal as serious fashion publications.

Owning and growing your own business is an all-consuming role. There is the day-to-day running of the business and also organising the social media aspect, which is demanding and an integral part of any business. You really have to love what you do and be completely authentic with what you create for your audience.

# *Amanda's* ADVICE

- Stay true to your aesthetic and make sure that your personality comes across in a genuine way; imagination and adventure are your key ingredients. So I feel it's best to embrace your individuality to stand out from the crowd.

*SOME
WOMEN
FEAR
THE FIRE.
SOME
SIMPLY
BECOME IT*

**R.H. SIN**

# MOTTO

*Courage doesn't always roar,
sometimes it is the little voice
at the end of the day that says,
'I will try again tomorrow.'*

# KRYSTAL BARTER

## FOUNDER OF THE PINK HOPE FOUNDATION

*Krystal Barter is the founder of the non-profit organisation Pink Hope, which aims to raise awareness and funding for hereditary breast and ovarian cancer, offering hope to thousands of women. She was a state finalist for the New South Wales Woman of the Year and author of* The Lucky One.

"I come from a family in which every woman had been diagnosed with breast and/or ovarian cancer. For a young woman, that is incredibly daunting. I literally didn't have a woman in my family who didn't have cancer.

When I was about eighteen, my mum and grandmother both tested positive for the BRCA1 gene mutation. At that time no one knew what it was. There simply wasn't much data or information to go by. So when I was tested as a 22-year-old new mum years later, it didn't really hit me until I started to research more about it, and only then did I realise what it meant for me. I literally carried the same gene mutation that killed or nearly killed every woman in my family – and it wasn't as if I could just remove it or say, 'No thanks, I don't want that gene mutation.' It was a part of me, inherited at birth. So I needed to take active steps to reduce my risk – from a certainty of cancer to as low as I could get it.

During that navigation and anxiety-ridden process, I saw the huge disparity between what was provided for women and families in my situation. The whole system was set up for people with cancer, but even though I didn't have cancer, I had the very real threat of it. So when I was feeling largely alone and incredibly isolated, I decided this would end with me and I would create Australia's first and only breast and ovarian preventative health organisation. It wasn't easy and was probably the hardest time in my life to embark on a venture which was not-for-profit – I was having a mastectomy and with two children under four ... Yep!

The biggest challenge I faced was that prevention really wasn't on many people's agenda. I was having more doors shut in my face than opened. And that can be incredibly frustrating when you are saying, 'I have been through it, I know what is needed, I know I can save lives right now. Help me.' But it was my dad who said that all the best and most worthwhile things in life take time. You need to believe in yourself, you need to believe that this is your path. I did believe it, and it seemed from that moment of my dad believing in me and believing I was the one who could change things, that the doors started to open.

I was able to get people to become involved by sharing my story and by being genuine. It's all about rallying around each other and empowering each other. We have the most amazing supporters from those who are influential, to my beautiful mum who has been right by my side. Our organisation is unique and has a mission that isn't the same as any other charity. People feel that and believe in the work we do.

## PINK HOPE IS BORN

When I first created Pink Hope, I was in a particular stage of my life. I was a young mum with a passion to change things. I wasn't experienced in not-for-profits, so I worked alongside a mentor and CEO of a leading not-for-profit, who showed and guided me with what should be done.

I came up with the name Pink Hope simply because pink is my favourite colour and 'hope' stood for the sentiment that I wanted women to receive from the work we do. The word 'hope' shows that you can be empowered and take control, while the butterfly symbolises transformation. Plus, it's my favourite creature. They go through something that dramatically changes them, from being a caterpillar to this beautiful creature. Kind of like what we hope to do for families who come to Pink Hope. The evolution of the organisation certainly hasn't happened overnight – I have personally learned so much.

Later, I was speaking at a conference at my old school and one of the ex-students was a book publisher and said, 'You know what, you have an incredible story – do you want to write a book?' You don't get that offer everyday! A big publisher jumped on board and signed me.

The cause received worldwide focus when Angelina Jolie put prevention and BRCA on the agenda with her story. Angelina has done so much for the cause globally

and for women's health. When I got to meet her, I couldn't get my words out. I felt like every BRCA sister was standing behind me, wanting to thank her and hug her. She truly is the most beautiful and remarkable woman ever. Brad Pitt was there as well, which was a bonus!

Take control of your risk of cancer. The dream for Pink Hope is to expand our sustainable funding so we can get back to saving lives and worrying less about where every dollar comes from. Over the next few years, as our funding increases, we want to employ another medical professional and have some more plans to expand our healthcare partnerships.

*SOMEDAY YOU WILL HAVE THE POWER TO MAKE A DIFFERENCE IN THE WORLD, SO USE IT WELL*

**MINDY KALING**

# MOTTO

*Give a woman the right makeup
and she can conquer the world!*

# CHARLOTTE TILBURY

## MAKEUP ARTIST, FOUNDER OF CHARLOTTE TILBURY

*An icon in the beauty industry, Charlotte Tilbury is responsible for some of our favourite red carpet looks on the world's most celebrated women. A makeup artist for more than twenty years, her passion for transforming faces has resulted in the creation of her cult beauty line, enabling every woman to have access to her makeup and beauty secrets.*

From the very beginning I've worked in the beauty industry. I have always believed in the magic and power of makeup, ever since I was a little girl. I understood the power of makeup for myself when I first applied mascara aged thirteen and instantly felt more empowered, confident and noticed. I've always been fascinated by the power a beautiful woman has when she enters a room and I wanted to understand that type of beauty and how its magnetic pull can command attention. I would study women's iconic faces obsessively to understand their beauty DNA. I taught myself how I could morph and cheat features to be bigger and brighter! A real turning point for me was meeting Mary Greenwell aged thirteen. I remember my parents' friends looking at a *Vogue* cover of Jerry Hall and saying: 'Look what Mary Greenwell has done!' She opened my eyes to the world of makeup. I became Mary's assistant, attended Glauca Rossi School of Make Up and the rest is history!

**BUILDING THE BRAND**

My first job was working with Kate Moss when we were both nineteen and kick-starting my career during the incredible supermodel era of the 80s and 90s, working with all the biggest names. Since then, I've worked with so many iconic actresses, models, and powerhouses –

from Kim Kardashian West, Cindy Crawford, Penélope Cruz, Salma Hayek, Gigi Hadid and Amal Clooney, to Jennifer Aniston, J. K. Rowling, Nicole Kidman and Olivia Culpo – the list is endless.

## THE INSPIRATION

I have so many female and male role models – they're hugely important. I have a mix of creatives, visionaries and rule breakers that I look to: Helena Rubinstein, Coco Chanel, Walt Disney, Steve Jobs, Winston Churchill, Estée Lauder… You need people who will make you dream and think outside the box! I call upon their energy and help to support me build my empire. I'm constantly learning from what they've achieved, how they thought differently and how they put their own ding in the universe.

I've grown up studying icons (such as Marilyn Monroe, Sophia Loren, Audrey Hepburn and Brigitte Bardot) by really analysing the structure of their faces. All these iconic women are role models for me in the sense that even though I was only looking at photos, they were teaching me how to make women more beautiful. They were giving me their beauty secrets! And obviously my mother is a great role model for me. She is so full of wisdom and anecdotes: 'The sun is beauty suicide,' and 'Lipstick is instant glamour!'

## THE CHALLENGES

People often ask me which challenges I have faced when launching my own brand and there have been a lot of difficult times over the past three and a half years. However, it really does depend on how you choose to perceive them.

From the very beginning I've always had a crystal clear image of how I've wanted my brand to be and the process of making that vision a reality hasn't always been easy. But I really believe in hard work and pushing yourself, because when you're passionate about something, anything is possible.

Rather than see those experiences as lows, I see them as opportunities and something to learn from. Self-belief is so important – it's just our insecurities that stop us and block us. When someone tells me 'No', I instantly think, 'It will be a "yes"!'

## THE LAUNCH

Realising my dreams by launching my own beauty brand was such a pivotal moment in my life. I actually came up with my brand idea at thirteen and it developed as I worked as a makeup artist for twenty-five years. I brought to life ten off-the-peg, colour-curated makeup wardrobe looks that

embodied the looks I originally created for all my celebrity clients: e.g. the Golden Goddess look for Jennifer Aniston and the Rock Chick look for Kate Moss. It's their incredible beauty DNA that I've extracted and encapsulated into my line. I'm now giving this exclusive red carpet ready makeup to everyone!

My vision for my brand has always been incredibly personal, magical and unique. I saw this blank space in the market for makeup that was easy to use and easy to choose, but that was also confidence-boosting and woman-to-woman. Women needed the daunting experience of shopping for and wearing makeup decoded.

I've only ever wanted to revolutionise and disrupt the beauty industry by launching only the very best products. If a product isn't an innovation or an invention then I'm not creating it. I won't create any 'me too' products. One of the first hero products that I launched was my miracle-working Magic Cream. I used to mix this backstage to turn around tired skin of super-models and celebrities and they became so obsessed with it they would ask me for my Magic Cream. It contains camellia oil, rosehip oil, Bio-nymph peptides and hyaluronic acid – instantly flooding the skin with moisture. I never apply makeup without it; it gives me the perfect glowing base.

The launch of my #GLOWMO range this summer is incredibly exciting – it's guaranteed to make you look and feel your most beautiful and glowing. This summer is all about glow moments and I wanted to create a range of products that would give you the most gorgeous, natural, enviable glow from dusk 'til dawn. From the Overnight Bronze & Glow mask that literally gives you the best tan of your life while you sleep, and my Beauty Glow palette for the most divine, flattering, beauty look, to my Unisex Healthy Glow tinted moisturiser, I've worked tirelessly to bring women products to enhance their natural beauty.

**SPREADING THE WORD**

Social media is so important to getting the word out there. I think the future of sharing beauty expertise and highlighting the latest makeup trends lies predominantly with the increasing rise of social media. It's about strategically using key platforms to share, showcase and simplify makeup looks that will dominate the beauty world over the coming seasons.

Social media will lead the way when it comes to informing and engaging with your consumers, as it allows you to break down key catwalk trends and take them from runway to reality. There are so many incredible beauty trends that I've referenced throughout awards season on the red carpet, only to be online literally seconds later. I love that I can do a look on Emma Roberts for the Oscars and share it instantly on Instagram (which has over 63 000 likes), but then the day after live stream the entire makeover to my fans through Facebook Live! Social media has given me my own magic media platforms. Facebook has now become one of my main video channels to broadcast live to thousands instantly (with 1.8 billion active monthly users) and Instagram is like having my own glossy publication and billboard (with 600 million active users).

Instagram has a huge impact on my work every day. It's an incredibly powerful tool in engaging your consumer in a deeper relationship than is possible instore, but also for expressing your brand DNA. It gives instant access to behind-the-scenes content and sharing artistry and expertise. It also gives me instant access to street-style beauty trends that I wouldn't normally see (such as the unicorn trend) and allows me to ask questions and much better understand my consumers' needs. By reading comments under posts I can work out which looks they love and the type of expert tricks they want to learn. I also love engaging my Instagram community in naming lipstick shades and making key suggestions for the brand!

# *Charlotte's* ADVICE

- I think success is about having a single-minded focus, visualising success, dreaming big, daring to make that dream a reality and self-belief. Life is limitless!

- Always reach for the stars. I always talk about the power of visualisation. Visualise what you want and don't give up until you get it!

# the GAME CHANGERS

## THE AUTHORS

# SAMANTHA BRETT

NEWS REPORTER, PRESENTER, BESTSELLING AUTHOR, COLUMNIST

"Moving from South Africa, where the post-apartheid violence was rampant, to Australia at a young age, I knew my parents had left everything behind to give us a better life and more opportunities. When I finished school, I knew I wanted to be in an industry that could bring stories of the world's struggle to local audiences and so I began studying Journalism and Law – which eventually led me to the career I enjoy now, being a news reporter at the Seven Network.

People think news reporting is glamorous because you are on television, but that is far from the reality. I will never forget the stories I have covered and the people I have met; from having to console families on the day their loved ones are murdered or unexpectedly die from car crashes, or drugs, or house fires; to sitting in gut-wrenching court cases watching people who have been tortured, raped, assaulted, or lost a loved one through someone else's negligence reliving the worst day of their lives. Or visiting someone whose home has just been ravished by floods or bushfires or a tornado. Or interviewing a mother who lost her baby due to medical negligence yet the law has done nothing to get her justice. I've followed around Prime Ministers from state to state during elections, reported from the front line of terror attacks, major world catastrophes and natural disasters, things I could never have fathomed as a university student learning my craft.

People often ask how to get into news reporting and the answer I always give is do as much work experience as possible. Back when I was studying, I worked for local newspapers, did behind the scenes work at television stations and then moved to New York to work at the Fox News Channel.

By the time I graduated, I was working for *Vogue* magazine and writing for the *Sunday Telegraph*, but I knew that

I wanted to make a difference. While I was living in New York, it was the era when *Sex and the City* came to the fore.

Everyone was talking about the newfound culture of celebrating female liberation and sexual independence, and I wanted to bring that discussion to Australia. I also wanted to do it in the format of a newfangled technology that had only just begun taking off: blogging. So, I called a newspaper in Australia and pitched my idea. There were only two blogs at that time: news and sport. Both were run by the newspaper and were steadily gaining momentum. At that point in time, no one dared run their own independent blog! Nonetheless, I knew an online forum on the modern perplexities of dating and mating would be a much needed addition not only to the newspaper, but to the wider community. The editors didn't completely agree. However, I wasn't deterred. Every week, for around six months, I would call the newspaper pitching my idea. Eventually, I moved back home to Sydney, and finally got the call I had been waiting for. 'You can start tomorrow,' they said, 'as long as you stop calling us!'

The first column gained 50 000 hits and thousands of comments, kicking off what no one (including my editor!) ever thought was possible. It became a worldwide hit, spawning TV shows, radio gigs and multiple bestselling books. After six years on the job and six books later, I was writing one of the most successful blogs in Australia – getting up to 100 000 readers per day, hundreds of comments and tens of thousands of dollars in endorsements, when I decided that instead of dishing out dating advice to the world, I wanted to get my own personal life on track and I wanted to return to the reason why I started journalism in the first place – because I'm a news junkie passionate about telling the stories that need to be heard. So I left the column that a million girls would dream of writing, and moved to the countryside to pursue my dream as a news reporter. I worked for Sky News which led me to file reports for CNN and CBS news, before returning to Sydney to work at the Seven Network.

Along the way, I have been inspired by some incredible women, many of whom you can read about in this book. Young women often come up to me and say 'I want to write a column like you' or have a book, or be a news presenter, and I always tell them the same thing: start now. Start from the very beginning, don't think you can take any shortcuts and always be the hardest working person in the room.

The women in this book, who have achieved far greater things than I could ever hope to achieve, all seem to share a similar sentiment: there are no easy paths to success. It really is about hard work – and loving every minute of the ride on the way to achieving your goals.

# SAM'S TIPS

• If you truly believe that you can achieve in something that you are passionate about, find a way to make it work. Whether that be moving city (or country), taking a new course, learning a new skill or finding a mentor, there is always a way.

• Read, read, read. Not just about people in your chosen field of work, but everything. The news, self-help books, inspirational stories – anything that will get your creative juices flowing.

• Do everything with honesty and integrity.

• Never be afraid to ask for a promotion.

• Be the hardest working person in the room.

• When one thing isn't working, switch gears!

*Photo credit: Chantal Bianchi. Dress: Carla Zampatti*

# STEPH ADAMS

EDITOR OF LAQUA MAGAZINE, BESTSELLING AUTHOR, ART DIRECTOR, INFLUENCER

Before I started working across international publications such as Net-a-Porter, *Elle*, British *Vogue*, *Harpers Bazaar* UK and *Conde Nast Traveller*, I was modelling internationally around the world in Europe, Asia and Australia.

I had completed a Bachelor of Arts in Graphic Design, Marketing and Psychology at Curtin University.

As a young teenager, I was never very good at school except for Art; I excelled at Art and by Year 11 and 12 had won two art awards.

At the age of sixteen at my mother's wedding, I was approached by a photographer to pursue modelling. It had never occurred to me but I took his advice and in the following year, fresh out of school, I started. My mother made me go to university while I was modelling as she didn't feel it was much of a career. As a young model, I felt very awkward amongst all the beautiful girls. I was tall with curly hair and freckles and very shy. Modelling gave me invaluable lessons on style, confidence, beauty and grooming which I have taken with me all my life.

In the summer of 2001, after a bad break-up, I left Perth and three days later I was on a plane to Europe to model in Germany. Louisa Models had previously been asking me but I had turned them down. Now I was there and I was prepared to give it everything I had. This experience changed the course of my life in such a positive way and an incredible journey never would have followed had that not have happened. Sometimes in life things happen that may feel devastating at the time, but you have to trust that life has a bigger plan for you, a better plan. I modelled with *Vogue* in Greece and various fashion magazines in Germany as well as doing commercials. I was in heaven and loving life. The people I was meeting and the experience taught me so much about who I was. On a shoot for *Vogue* in Greece, I met the Art Director on set, a very stylish woman. I remember being quite intrigued by her job and her creative ability and wondered if I could do the same thing.

When I moved to Sydney from Perth the following year, it never occurred to me to try and get a job in magazines and publishing, even though that was what I was being drawn to. I had applied to over thirty advertising agencies in Sydney only to be turned down as I had no experience, when FPC Magazines finally came calling after they had seen a mock-up of a magazine layout I had done at university. FPC Magazines housed all the major magazines at the time from *Vogue* Australia, *Vogue Living*, *GQ* and many more. I was brought in to design across eight of them including *Vogue*. After a few weeks on the job, I knew I had found what it was I was meant to be doing. From there I went on to Art Direct for *Marie Claire* magazine in Promotions, working with the large beauty and fashion brands such as L'Oréal and winning some major accounts in the advertising department. I also worked with *Harper's Bazaar*, *Grazia*, *InStyle*, *Belle*, *Vogue Living*, *Vogue Entertaining and Travel* and *Gourmet Traveller*.

In 2007, I started www.stephadamscreative.com.au alongside working with magazines. I would return home from a long work day only to start on another design project at home. I was starting to get a lot of great clients such as Leeuwin Estate, Aravina Estate, Face Plus Medispa and more. I was creating logos, brochures, skincare labels, packaging and everything in between.

Another turning point in my career just happened to be when I met my husband on Darling Point Road at a New Years Eve party in Sydney in 2008. He was living in London and invited me to a wedding in South Africa. A few months later we had various dates in London and Paris and four months later we were engaged. It was a whirlwind romance!

When I moved to London I started to work for *Marie Claire*, *Harper's Bazaar*, *Elle* and then British *Vogue* asked me to come in and see my folio. The Creative Director said she loved all my work and would love to take me on but they had no budget. I offered to work for free for a week and then they kept me on after that. I took in everything and meeting the lovely Stephen Quinn and hearing his stories from when he launched *GQ* was a 'pinch me' moment. From there I then went to work for Net-a-Porter. I was brought in to design the first ever magazine with Claudia Schiffer on the front. It took three months to design their entire magazine from front to back. Working with Natalie Massenet and the whole creative team was a dream come true and an unforgetable experience.

On our return to Sydney, I started interviewing different celebrities about their brands as well as my clients across www.stephadams.com, which I had started in 2009. I was attending events and travelling all over the world, posting my experiences. It was early days and it was before anyone in Australia really understood the power of blogs. Over the years, I started to collaborate more and more with various brands such as Dior, SK-II, L'Oréal, Sheridan, Waterford Crystal, Estée Lauder and many charities.

I was still designing when a client came along and asked for a coffee table book to be designed around luxurious hotels and spas across the globe. The experience gave me more confidence in dealing with different hotels and PR companies. I then formed my next partnership: *Good to Glow*. In 2015, along with my co-author, we put together a healthy recipe book from different celebrities and hotels around the world. It was a year and a half before we found a publisher: teNeues Publishing produced the book in April, 2016. Just as this was being

finished a new book idea was forming with my current co-author, Samantha Brett: *The Game Changers*. We published it together in December 2016. We never imagined the success that would come from the first edition. In July 2017 I launched Laqua magazine, an online magazine dedicated to beauty, fashion and lifestyle.

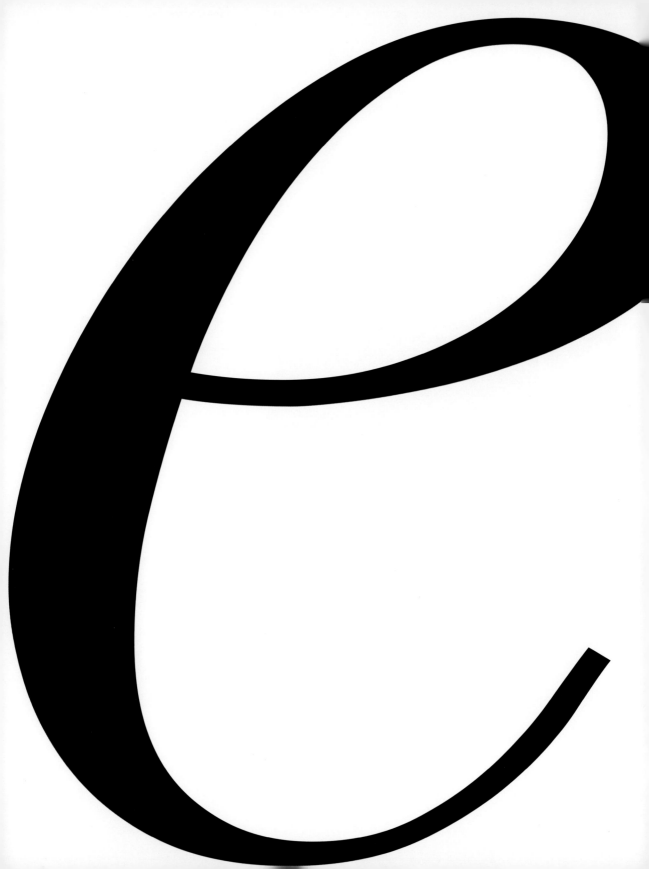

# EPILOGUE

Ladies, this isn't the end, but just the beginning of your journey towards achieving your goals. The Game Changers are not just the women you've read about in these pages – they are all around you, in everyday life. They are your best friends, neighbours, sisters, co-workers, mums, daughters. They are the everyday women following their dreams and enjoying the journey, rather than putting too much emphasis on the destination. Every woman's story is different; every journey is varied. Every passion is unique, and it's this uniqueness that we hope will be celebrated by you, and celebrated by the world around you.

If we can leave you with anything, it's this: don't be afraid. Get up and do it. Change the things about your life you feel are letting you down. Get inspiration from books, film, art, travel, volunteering, giving back and continually expanding your mind. And know that one voice, one action, one belief – yours – can make all the difference.

# THE AUTHORS

Samantha Brett is a news reporter and the bestselling author of six books.

Samantha began her journalism career in New York at the Fox News Channel, before return to Sydney to write Australia's number-one lifestyle column for six years.

Samantha has since gone on to file news reports for Sky News, CBS, CNN, and currently works for Australia's Seven Network. Samantha has covered a variety of international stories and breaking news.

Samantha has written more than 1000 articles for newspapers and magazines around the world on a variety of topics. She is passionate about helping other women to achieve their dreams, and is a proud supporter of the Pink Hope Foundation.

*Instagram: @samantha_brett*
*www.samanthabrett.com*

Steph Adams is a bestselling author, the editor and founder of Laqua Magazine, an art director and an influencer. Born in Perth, Western Australia, Steph began her career in the fashion industry as an international model before moving to Sydney in 2003. She graduated with a Bachelor of Arts from Curtin University in 2004 and started working as an art director for *Vogue*, *Vogue Living*, *Marie Claire*, *InStyle*, *Grazia*, *GQ*, *Belle*, *Gourmet Traveller*, *House and Garden* and *Delicious* magazine. Steph moved to London in 2009 and worked as an art editor for Net-a-Porter, designing their first-ever magazine with Claudia Schiffer on the front. She has since worked internationally with British *Vogue*, *Elle*, *Harper's Bazaar*, *Condé Nast Traveler* and *Marie Claire*.

As an art director, Steph has collaborated with some of the industry's most iconic image-makers including Stephen Quinn (Publisher of British *Vogue*) and Net-a-Porter founder Natalie Massenet.

In April of 2016, Steph co-authored her first book, a collection of healthy recipes from celebrities, hotels, spas and cafés around the world, called *Good to Glow*, which was released by teNeues Publishing. The book has since been translated into three languages and has been published in Germany, UK, US and France.

Steph has worked professionally with Dior, SK-II, Estée Lauder, WelleCo, Aerin Lauder, L'Oréal Paris, Sheridan, Waterford Crystal and many more.

*Awards: Australia's Top 50 Influencer Award, 2017*

**Instagram: @stephadams2012**
**www.stephadams.com**
**www.stephadamscreative.com.au**

# ACKNOWLEDGEMENTS

This incredible journey started as a thought bubble on a plane with my husband, Ben, by my side, and it was cemented during one of the many morning walks I enjoy with my friend and inspiration Steph Adams. The women we contacted were instantly drawn to our idea to put their beautiful stories of inspiration and success into a coffee table book that would not only be enjoyed by women around the world, but would help highlight the wonderful work carried out by the Pink Hope Foundation as well. I'd like to thank these two special people in my life, along with my parents, Jon and Alice, and my brother, Dale, for always championing me. To my girlfriends who are always there to lend a loving ear, to everyone at Channel Seven for their support and love, and to all the inspirational women who've given up their valuable time and tips to participate in our book: thank you.

**SAMANTHA BRETT**

Firstly, I would like to thank all the inspiring women in our book who have generously donated their time in telling their story. Thanks also to my business partner and friend, Samantha Brett, who has constantly been an inspiration in my life, and to all the people who are constantly inspiring me each day: my mum and family, and my really good friends who have stuck by me no matter what. In the end it's all about the journey. Be kind, don't compare yourself to anyone, at the end of the day follow your heart, do what you love and give back any way you can because life is too short for anything else. To all the others who have been generous enough to donate their time, thank you.

**STEPH ADAMS**